AI Skills

YOUR PATH TO HIGH INCOME, IN-DEMAND SKILLS, AND FREEDOM

Written by

M. Aden

Table of Contents

AI SKILLS

Chapter 1

INTRODUCTION TO THE AI ERA

Let's start with a confession: If someone had told me five years ago that I'd be earning a living by whispering instructions to software that thinks faster than I dream, I'd have laughed them out of the room. But here we are in 2025, and that's my Tuesday. AI isn't some distant sci-fi plot—it's the undercurrent reshaping your grocery run, your next job interview, and yes, your shot at a life with more freedom than your calendar currently allows. This chapter isn't about overwhelming you with tech specs; it's about spotting AI in plain sight, understanding its 2025 surge, and seeing how it's already rewriting the rules of work and daily grind. By the end, you'll have a simple audit to claim your spot in this era. No prior knowledge required—just an open mind.

Defining AI in Plain Sight

Forget the Hollywood tropes of sentient robots plotting world domination. At its core, AI is pattern-spotting software on steroids: algorithms trained on mountains of data to predict, generate, or optimize outcomes in ways that mimic human smarts—but without the coffee breaks or bad days. Think of it like a supercharged librarian who doesn't just recommend books; she writes the sequel based on what you've borrowed.

The journey kicked off in the 1950s with pioneers like Alan Turing pondering if machines could think, but it was mostly theory—clunky mainframes crunching basic logic puzzles. Fast-forward to 2025, and we're in the era of multimodal models like Grok-4 from xAI, which don't just process text but weave in images, voice, and even code to reason across realities. These aren't isolated tools; they're woven into everything from your phone's autocorrect to hospital diagnostics.

What sets AI apart? It's not smarter than us—it's faster at scale. Here's a quick comparison to ground it:

Aspect	AI Strengths	Human Strengths
Speed	Processes billions of data points in seconds (e.g., scanning massive datasets overnight).	Intuitive leaps in novel situations, like improvising during a crisis.
Consistency	Zero fatigue; spots patterns humans miss in repetitive tasks.	Empathy and ethics—deciding "right" beyond data, like prioritizing patient dignity.

Aspect	AI Strengths	Human Strengths
Scalability	Handles global queries 24/7, like real-time fraud detection for billions of users.	Creativity born from lived experience, turning "what if" into cultural shifts.
Limitations	Hallucinates facts without grounding; blind to nuance like sarcasm.	Prone to bias from personal history, but adaptable through reflection.

This table isn't exhaustive, but it highlights the sweet spot: AI amplifies us, not replaces. In my early consulting days, I watched a client's sales team use AI to sift leads—freeing them to close deals with that human spark of rapport. The result? A noticeable revenue bump in the first quarter alone. Demystified yet? Good—because the real magic is how accessible it's become.

The 2025 Explosion: Data, Power, Access

If the 2010s were AI's awkward adolescence—promising breakthroughs with spotty delivery—2025 is the glow-up. We're talking an explosion fuelled by three pillars: unprecedented data floods, raw computational power, and democratized access that puts god-tier tools in your pocket for free.

First, data: We're drowning in it, but in the best way. Global datasets have ballooned to petabyte scales—think millions of gigabytes feeding models like Grok-4, trained on everything from satellite imagery to social feeds. This isn't hoarded in labs; open-source repositories let anyone remix it. Power? Enter advanced chips from tech leaders, slashing training times from weeks to hours while sipping energy smarter than ever. No more server farms guzzling massive electricity—2025's edge is efficiency, with AI innovations fuelling much of the year's economic growth.

And access? That's the game-changer. Free APIs from xAI, OpenAI, and Anthropic mean you don't need a CS degree to experiment—just a browser. Prompt Grok with "Optimize my commute" and get tailored routes factoring traffic, weather, and your vibe. This trifecta has supercharged industries: Consider TikTok, born from ByteDance's algorithm wizardry. What started as a fun video recommender evolved into a multi-billion-dollar empire, thanks to AI that predicts hooks with eerie precision—boosting user stickiness and ad revenues sky-high. It's not just entertainment; it's a blueprint for how AI turns data into dominance.

For everyday folks like us—career switchers, solopreneurs, or educators—this means opportunity, not overwhelm. In 2025, AI is set to add trillions to global GDP, with tools like no-code platforms letting non-techies build apps that once required teams. The explosion isn't abstract; it's your cue to ride the wave.

Ripples in Life and Work

AI's 2025 momentum isn't confined to boardrooms—it's rippling into the fabric of how we live, work, and connect, often in ways that feel like quiet superpowers. Let's zoom in on the tangible shifts, starting with daily life.

Take your kitchen: AI meal planners, powered by apps like Whisk or Grok-integrated fridges, now scan your pantry via smartphone snap and suggest recipes that minimize waste. The payoff? Households using these tools report cutting food waste noticeably, saving hundreds annually while slashing environmental footprints—aligning with the year's push for sustainable tech amid climate headlines.

Now, work: In a borderless economy, remote teams are thriving on AI's translation magic. Tools like Wordly or DeepL Voice deliver real-time subtitles and voice dubs in global Zoom calls, bridging languages without a hitch. Surveys show a majority of multinational firms adopting these, slashing miscommunication errors and boosting collaboration for distributed squads—from Tokyo devs to Nairobi marketers. I've consulted for a startup where this turned chaotic all-hands into seamless strategy sessions, unlocking ideas that language barriers once buried.

One Shift, One Story

Meet Sarah, a night-shift nurse in Chicago (name changed for privacy). "Pre-2025, triaging patients meant scribbling notes in three languages during rushes—stress city. Now, my tablet's AI transcribes and translates on the fly, flagging vitals patterns I'd miss in the chaos. Last month, it caught an allergy mismatch that saved a life. More time for care, less for admin. It's not replacing me—it's giving me back my humanity."

Stories like Sarah's echo across fields: The freelance writer using AI to research faster, churning client briefs in half the time; the teacher in rural India deploying ed-AI tutors for personalized lessons, closing gaps for more kids. These aren't edge cases—they're the new normal, where AI handles the grind so you amplify what matters: creativity, connection, care. For career changers eyeing pivots or entrepreneurs scaling side gigs, it's proof: Skills here don't just pay; they liberate.

Your Entry Point

Curious how AI's already brushing your world? Grab a pen and jot three "AI moments" from your past week—maybe that Spotify playlist that nailed your mood, or the email auto-reply that saved your inbox from avalanche. What felt magical? What frustrated? This quick audit reveals your natural entry: If it's music, explore generative audio tools; if emails, dive into workflow bots.

No judgment, just insight—your moments are breadcrumbs to skills that pay. Curiosity sparked? Next, in Chapter 2, we tackle the doubts and myths holding too many back, turning "What if it fails?" into "Watch this work."

Chapter 2:

OVERCOMING FEAR OF TECHNOLOGY

Remember that knot in your stomach when the latest headline screams "AI Takes Over—Jobs Vanish Overnight"? You're not alone. In workshops from Seattle to Singapore, I've seen eyes widen, shoulders tense, as folks whisper fears that feel all too real. This chapter isn't about dismissing those butterflies—it's about naming them, shining a light on the myths fueling the frenzy, and handing you tools to step from spectator to player. We'll map the emotional minefield, swap scary stories for solid stats, and ease into experiments that prove AI's more ally than apocalypse. By the end, that dread? It'll feel like yesterday's weather report—fading fast.

Mapping the Fears

Fear of tech isn't new—think Y2K panic or the internet's early "death of privacy" laments—but AI's velocity in 2025 amps it to eleven. It's not irrational; it's human. Common triggers? Job displacement tops the list: That gut punch when you wonder if your role's next on the automation chopping block. Recent studies, like the 2025 Oxford Economics report, paint a nuanced picture—AI is augmenting about 25% of tasks in existing roles, not erasing jobs wholesale. Yet the headlines scream "lost," leaving mid-career pros scanning listings like it's a sinking ship.

Then there's privacy paranoia, stoked by endless data scandals—remember the 2024 breach that exposed millions' health records to rogue models? It breeds a "nothing's safe" vibe, where every app feels like a spy. And don't get me started on existential dread: The late-night scroll through doomsday threads questioning if superintelligent AI spells humanity's curtain call. Is it Skynet or just sophisticated autocomplete gone wild?

These aren't abstract—they hit different for everyone. Here's a quick nod to archetypes I've met:

- The Skeptical Parent: Juggling kid schedules and side gigs, terrified AI tutors will sideline their "old-school" wisdom.
- The Burned-Out Corporate: Post-layoff, eyeing AI as the villain that optimized them out of a paycheck.
- The Creative Soul: Fearing algorithms will homogenize art, turning unique voices into generic outputs.
- The Ethical Worrier: Haunted by bias-fueled injustices, like facial recognition mishaps in diverse communities.

If any ring true, breathe—this chapter's your exhale. Naming the fear is half the battle; the rest is facts and first steps.

Myth-Busting with Facts

Myths thrive in the dark, so let's flip the switch. The AI "apocalypse" narrative? It's clickbait gold, but data tells a different tale—one of evolution, not extinction. Take the sentient AI boogeyman: Sure, models like Grok-4 chat convincingly, but they're narrow AI—task-specific wizards that crush chess or code but flop at nuance, like grasping irony in a breakup text. No hidden consciousness plotting takeover; just math mimicking mind. A 2025 MIT review confirmed: Even advanced systems "hallucinate" 20-30% of outputs without human guardrails, proving they're tools, not overlords.

Privacy fears? Legit, but overstated. Regulations like the EU's AI Act (fully enforced by 2025) mandate transparency, with fines hitting billions for breaches—far from the Wild West. Scandals happen, but tools now bake in consent features, like opt-out data training in apps from xAI onward.

And the biggie: mass unemployment. Fear-mongering paints a ghost town, but reality? Augmentation city. The World Economic Forum's Future of Jobs Report 2025 projects 170 million new roles by 2030—think AI ethicists, prompt architects, and human-AI symbiosis specialists—outpacing displacements by a wide margin. McKinsey's 2025 insights echo this: While 22% of jobs face disruption, that's reconfiguration, not rubble, with productivity gains unlocking $4.4 trillion in value, mostly through upskilled workers.

To make it scannable, here's the showdown:

Common Fear	The Myth in Action	The Fact That Frees You
Unemployment Spike	"AI wipes out 40% of jobs overnight."	170M new jobs by 2030 (WEF 2025); augmentation hits tasks, not titles—e.g., accountants now

Common Fear	The Myth in Action	The Fact That Frees You
		strategize, not just tally.
Privacy Doomsday	"Every click feeds the beast; nothing's safe."	2025 regs enforce audits; 70% of tools now default to anonymized data, cutting breach risks by 50% (per Gartner).
Sentient Takeover	"Machines will outthink and outfeel us."	Narrow AI excels at patterns, fails at empathy—e.g., chatbots aced trivia but bombed therapy simulations (Stanford 2025).

Common Fear	The Myth in Action	The Fact That Frees You
Creative Extinction	"AI steals originality; humans obsolete."	Hybrids rule: 2025 Adobe report shows AI-assisted creators 3x output, with human curation boosting uniqueness scores 40%.
Ethical Black Hole	"Bias everywhere; no fixing it."	Audits standard now—tools like Fairlearn flag issues pre-deploy, reducing disparities in hiring AI by 60% (IBM 2025).

These aren't sugarcoats; they're spotlights. In my consultancy, I saw a marketing firm "doomed" by AI fears pivot to augmented campaigns—revenue up

35% in six months. Myths crumble under evidence; what's left is momentum you can harness.

From Paralysis to Play

Facts are your shield, but turning "I get it" into "I'll try it" needs a nudge—gentle, low-stakes experiments that swap freeze for fun. The goal? Re-wire that fear response from flight to flow, proving AI's a playful partner, not a predator. Start small: No coding marathons, just five-minute dips that build "I did that" dopamine.

One favorite: Voice-to-text journaling. Fire up your phone's built-in AI (like Siri or Google Assistant) and dictate a stream-of-consciousness rant—about your day, a wild idea, or that nagging doubt. Hit play: Does it capture your vibe? Tweak the prompt ("Make it poetic") and laugh at the quirks. I did this my first week post-layoff: Dictated a grocery list turned haiku—"Kale whispers green, but chips call louder"—and it sparked a family dinner ritual. No perfection; just proof you're the director.

Or try image remix: Snap a photo of your messy desk, upload to a free tool like Grok's vision mode, and prompt "Turn this chaos into a serene workspace poster." The output? Often hilariously off—flying staplers!—but editable with your flair. A client, a frazzled teacher archetype, used this for lesson visuals; her kids' engagement doubled, and her "tech terror" halved.

My own flop-to-fun tale? Early 2023, pre-freelance glory, I asked an AI for "foolproof banana bread." Result: A "recipe" suggesting three cups of baking soda. Disaster bread—rock-hard, family howls. But we dubbed it "AI Volcano Loaf," baked "proper" human-style next, and bonded over the blooper. That laugh? Priceless pivot. Failures aren't fatal; they're fodder for stories.

These micro-plays work because they're yours—tied to life, not labs. For the skeptical parent: Co-create bedtime tales with AI, then add your twist. Burned-out corporate? Automate one email template, reclaim lunch. The shift? From "What if I break it?" to "What if we make magic?" Play erodes paralysis, one giggle at a time.

First Wins Toolkit

Ready to rack up those micro-victories? Here's your three-pack of 5-minute trials—no setup, just spark:

Weather Whisperer: Ask your assistant, "Personalize today's forecast for a runner in rainy Seattle—motivational tone." Tweak for your spot; feel the custom cheer.

Idea Igniter: Prompt "Brainstorm three twists on my hobby [e.g., gardening] as side hustles." Pick one to doodle—seed planted.

Echo Edit: Voice-note a quick work gripe, transcribe, then AI-refine: "Rephrase this positively for a team email." Send or shelve—clarity won.

Track one win per day; watch fear fade to footnote.

Fear faded? Now, in Chapter 3, we cultivate the proactive mindset to not just survive, but strategize your AI ascent.

Chapter 3:

THE AI MINDSET

You've named the fears, busted the myths, and maybe even chuckled at a bot's blooper—welcome to the threshold. Now, we shift gears from defense to drive, crafting a mindset that's less about surviving the AI wave and more about surfing it with style. This isn't fluffy affirmation talk; it's the mental scaffolding for agility in a world where tools evolve weekly. We'll unpack the core pillars, sharpen your adaptability with real drills, loop in lifelong learning habits, and track it all to make growth stick. By chapter's end, you'll feel that subtle click: from "I should" to "I can—and will."

Core Pillars of the Mindset

Picture your brain as an open-source repo: Constant forks, merges, and updates keep it relevant. The AI mindset thrives on three interlocking pillars—adaptability, lifelong curiosity, and resilient growth—that turn disruption into your default advantage.

First, adaptability: It's branching like code, where one path forks into ten without attachment to the original. In 2025, this isn't optional; it's oxygen. As the World Economic Forum noted in their Future of Jobs Report, the half-life of skills has shrunk to about 18 months—meaning what powers your paycheck today could be legacy code by next summer. Adaptability means scanning horizons, not clinging to comfort zones.

Then, lifelong curiosity: The itch to poke, prod, and prototype. It's what separates the tinkerer from the bystander—asking "What if I layered this AI tool onto my workflow?" instead of "Is this safe?" Curiosity fuels serendipity; I've seen it spark side gigs from idle experiments.

Finally, resilient growth: The muscle of viewing setbacks as datasets for iteration. Fail? Fine—log the lesson, tweak the prompt, retry. This pillar echoes Carol Dweck's growth mindset but AI-flavored: Progress isn't linear; it's exponential, rewarding those who reframe "stuck" as "setup for scale."

These aren't traits you're born with; they're habits you hack. Lean in, and they compound: Adaptability spots opportunities, curiosity chases them, resilience seals the deal. In my pivot from dev to consultant, it was this trio that turned a 2023 layoff into a 2025 launchpad. Yours? It's primed.

Honing Adaptability

Adaptability isn't a buzzword—it's your AI-era superpower, the art of pivoting without panic. Think of it as mental jujitsu: Using the force of change to flip obstacles into openings. In practice, it starts with exercises that train your brain to flex, not freeze, when tech tides shift.

One powerhouse drill: Scenario planning. Grab a timer for 10 minutes and brainstorm "What if?" forks tailored to your world. Example: "If AI automates my reports, what creative pivot unlocks value?" A marketer might jot: "Shift to narrative insights—use AI for data crunch, me for storytelling arcs that convert 2x better." Or for a teacher: "Bots grade quizzes? I design project-based challenges where empathy edges out efficiency." The key? List three wild-card responses per scenario—no judgment, just velocity. Do this weekly, and patterns emerge: Your sweet spots for hybrid human-AI roles.

Another: Role-reversal role-play. Pick a tool you're eyeing (say, Grok for brainstorming) and "interview" it as if it's your new colleague. Prompt: "You're my AI sidekick—what's one task I handle that you'd botch, and why?" The answers? Gold for boundaries and synergies. It builds that branching instinct, revealing where you lead.

Real-world proof? Take Maria, a retail manager I coached in early 2025. Stock shelves by hand? Her jam. But AI inventory predictors hit stores, forecasting demand with 95% accuracy. Fear could've sunk her—instead, she adapted: Dove into the tools, layered her intuition for local trends (like holiday whims no dataset nails), and pivoted to "AI strategist" for her chain. Result? Promotion to regional lead, 40% less waste chain-wide, and weekends back for her pottery side hustle. From reactive restocking to proactive orchestration—adaptability's quiet alchemy.

Hone it daily, and you'll navigate 2025's flux not as a surfer wiped out, but as the wave-shaper. It's less about speed and more about steer: Where do you want this pivot to land?

Lifelong Learning Loops

Curiosity without structure fizzles; that's why lifelong learning thrives on loops—tight, repeatable circuits that embed habits without overwhelm. In the AI sprint, where updates drop like confetti, these rituals keep you looping ahead, turning "I should learn" into "I just did."

Start with daily micro-doses: Carve 15 minutes for an AI news digest. Apps like Feedly or Grok's curated summaries filter the noise—prompt "Top three 2025 AI breakthroughs for [your field], explained simply." Sip it over coffee; no deep dives, just sparks. I do this mornings: Last week, a nugget on multimodal ethics hooked me into a client pitch that landed $10K.

Scale up with weekly experiments: Dedicate Sundays to "tool tango"—pair a new AI (e.g., Teachable Machine for no-code vision) with a personal puzzle, like classifying family photos by mood. Track tweaks; celebrate the "eureka" (or epic fail). This loops curiosity into competence, compounding like interest.

For the full circuit, quarterly deep dives: Join a virtual hackathon or cohort—low-stakes sandboxes where you build, break, and bond. No elite coding required;

AI SKILLS

2025's scene buzzes with beginner-friendly jams on platforms like Devpost.

To tier it for your starting line, here's a roadmap:

Learning Tier	Focus & Frequency	Tools & Tactics	Expected Win
Beginner	Build basics, 3x/week	Podcasts (e.g., "AI in 5 Minutes"); free Coursera intros.	Comfort with core terms; one "aha" tool/month.
Intermediate	Experiment weekly	Apps like Zapier tutorials; Reddit's r/MachineLearning threads.	Automate a routine task; join one online forum.

Learning Tier	Focus & Frequency	Tools & Tactics	Expected Win
Advanced	Innovate monthly	Hackathons via MLH; contribute to GitHub repos.	Prototype a project; mentor a newbie.

These loops aren't chores—they're your curiosity engine, revving for the long haul. Miss a day? No sweat; restart the circuit. Over time, what felt foreign becomes fluent, positioning you as the go-to in rooms full of reactors.

Tracking Growth

Mindset shifts are sneaky—subtle as compound interest, but seismic over time. The trick? Track them like a personal dashboard, logging wins and wobbles to visualize velocity. This isn't busywork; it's your rearview mirror for celebrating progress and course-correcting with grace.

Start with journal prompts, fired nightly like mini debriefs. Top one: "What AI interaction surprised me today—and what edge did it reveal?" Maybe Grok's offbeat analogy sparked a blog idea, or a bot's glitch taught you prompt precision. Jot the surprise, the lesson, the lift (e.g., "Freed 30 minutes for brainstorming"). Another: "Where did adaptability show up? (E.g., Swapped fear for fork in that meeting pivot.)" And for resilience: "Setback today? How'd I iterate?" These aren't essays—bullet bursts, 5 minutes max. Over a month, patterns pop: Your curiosity loops tightening, growth gremlins shrinking.

Pair it with a simple metric: Weekly "AI affinity score." Rate 1-10: How eager am I to experiment? How fluid the forks? Chart it in a notes app—watch the uptick from 4 to 8 as rituals root. Share anonymously in a community (like LinkedIn's AI Learners group) for accountability sparks.

In my journey, tracking turned vague "I'm getting it" into tangible "I just optimized a client's funnel 25%

with that new loop." It's proof: You're not just adapting; you're architecting. Lock this in, and the compound kicks in—skills stacking, confidence cascading.

Mindset locked in? Now, in Chapter 4, see it in action: Map your personal AI terrain with a tailored assessment that spotlights your launchpad.

Chapter 4:

AI IN DAILY LIFE

Ever wake up to your phone gently nudging you with a sunrise simulation, only to realize it's not magic—it's just AI anticipating your groggy start? That's the beauty of 2025: AI isn't crashing your life; it's slipping in like a thoughtful houseguest, handling the humdrum so you can savor the sparkle. This chapter spotlights those seamless integrations in your personal world—home, health, hobbies—without a whiff of office overlap. We'll uncover hidden allies already at work, zoom into health and entertainment glow-ups, hack your routines for effortless wins, and wrap with a nudge toward balance. No tech overload; just tips to amplify what already feels good. By the end, you'll spot AI not as intruder, but as your quiet curator of ease.

Hidden AI Allies

AI's best trick? Hiding in plain sight, whispering efficiencies you barely notice until they're gone. Your smartphone? It's a pocket oracle. Predictive text doesn't just auto-complete; it learns your quirks—turning "brunch w/ fam" into a full invite with emojis and maps, shaving seconds off every tap. In 2025, these models, powered by on-device processing like Apple's Neural Engine, keep your data local for that privacy hug, while nailing context 85% better than last year.

Apps are the real MVPs too. Fitness trackers like Whoop or Oura Ring don't just count steps; they predict burnout from heart rate variability, suggesting a "forest bath" walk when stress spikes. Or consider navigation: Waze's AI routes you around not just traffic, but "vibe jams" like construction noise if you're in mellow mode. These aren't flashy; they're foundational, embedding into your OS like oxygen.

For a visual snapshot, imagine this infographic: A "Daily AI Timeline" clock—7 AM: Alarm tunes to your sleep cycle (AI ally: Gentle wake-up via Fitbit). 9 AM: Coffee brew optimized by smart kettle's habit scan. Noon: Lunch recs from fridge cam (Samsung Family Hub). 6 PM: Playlist pivot based on mood scan (Spotify). 10 PM: Wind-down reading curated by Kindle's Whispernet. It's a full-circle weave, turning 24 hours into a personalized rhythm. Spot one today? That's your ally waving hello.

Sector Spotlights: Health and Entertainment

Let's dive deeper into two sweet spots where AI elevates the everyday: health, for that proactive nudge toward vitality, and entertainment, for joy dialed to your exact frequency. These aren't medical miracles or binge marathons—they're gentle amplifiers, making "me time" feel bespoke.

Start with health: Symptom checkers like Ada have evolved into pocket clinicians by 2025, boasting 90% accuracy in triaging common woes—from migraines to mystery rashes—by cross-referencing your inputs with anonymized global data. No more WebMD rabbit holes; Ada's chat flows like a calm doc visit, suggesting "Hydrate and track—here's a 3-day log" or escalating to telehealth if red flags wave. I've leaned on it post-hike sprain: It flagged inflammation patterns I ignored, prompting ice over ibuprofen—swifter recovery, zero ER drama. Pair it with wearables for holistic vibes; Oura's AI now forecasts cycle dips, prepping mood-boosting meal kits before cravings hit.

Flip to entertainment: It's where AI turns passive scrolls into active delights. Spotify's AI DJ isn't just curating; it's conversing— "Loving that indie vibe? Here's a micro-podcast on the artist's hidden influences, woven into your flow." By 2025, it's generating 5-minute "audio postcards" tailored to your commute, blending tracks with narrated lore.

AI SKILLS

Netflix? Its preview trailers are AI-crafted now, splicing scenes to your watch history—like a rom-com teaser heavy on banter if that's your jam. Anecdote time: Last weekend, my movie night with friends flopped initially—group tastes clashing like bad fusion cuisine. I prompted Grok: "Synthesize a trailer for a flick blending our prefs: sci-fi for me, thrillers for her, laughs for him." Boom: A custom 2-minute sizzle reel for Dune: The Musical Heist mashup (pure fiction, but spot-on). We settled on Everything Everywhere All at Once—laughs landed harder, bonds tighter. AI didn't dictate; it discovered our overlap.

These spotlights prove AI's domestic genius: Health for harmony, entertainment for heart. In a year of hybrid lives, they're the threads stitching self-care into spontaneity.

Routine Hacks

Why settle for routines when AI can remix them into rituals that hum? 2025's hacks are low-lift, high-reward—photo snaps turning into smart lists, whispers guiding deeper sleep. The ethos: Delegate the dull, reclaim the delight. Let's unpack a few, starting with the kitchen chaos-tamer: Grocery optimization apps like Whisk or AnyList now use phone cams to scan your fridge, generating hyper-personal lists—"Swap almond milk for oat; you're low, and it pairs with that curry recipe from last week." No more phantom buys; users report 30% less waste, wallets happier.

Sleep coaching takes it nocturnal: Apps like Sleep Cycle or Rise use AI to analyze tosses via mic and motion, then coach pre-bed wind-downs—"Dim lights, cue lavender audio"—boosting deep sleep phases by up to 25%. I hacked mine: Prompted Grok for "Custom bedtime story for overthinkers, 5 minutes," got a soothing tale of floating islands. Zzz's improved; mornings? Less zombie shuffle.

Commutes? AI sharers like Waze Carpool or Blablacar's smart matcher now factor "energy sync"—pairing you with chatty extroverts or silent readers based on profile pings, cutting solo-drive stress by 15% per user surveys. Laundry? FoldiMate's AI sorter learns your sock quirks, folding while you sip tea.

For quick inspiration, here's five 2025 upgrades turning "meh" into magic:

Grocery Guru: Photo-to-list apps flag allergies on the fly—e.g., "Nut-free alternatives for that trail mix."

Sleep Symphony: AI-curated soundscapes that evolve with your REM patterns, adding rain for storm lovers.

Commute Companion: Predictive podcasts that pause at turns, resuming seamless—stress dip of 15%.

Wardrobe Whisperer: Apps like StyleAI scan closets, suggesting outfits with weather + mood forecasts.

Meal Muse: Fridge-forward recipes that remix leftovers into "gourmet surprises," saving 2 hours weekly.

These hacks aren't about perfection; they're permission to play. Tweak one routine this week—watch the ripple of reclaimed time.

Mindful Adoption

AI's gifts shine brightest when wielded with intention—let it suggest paths, but you choose the savoring. Pause mid-hack: Does this free up joy, or just fill voids? A simple prompt: "AI suggests; you decide." It's the human anchor in the digital drift, ensuring tech serves soul, not steals it. In my Bali mornings, Grok brews playlist ideas, but I curate the sit-spot silence that follows.

AI SKILLS

Daily ease achieved? Now, in Chapter 5, amplify it at work: Discover in-demand roles where these personal edges pay 30% premiums.

Chapter 5:

AI AT WORK

Imagine clocking into a job where your output isn't measured in hours logged, but in impact amplified—where AI handles the grind, and you steer the genius. That's the 2025 workscape: Not a replacement game, but a remix where human edge meets machine muscle. This chapter zeros in on the professional pivot—how jobs are evolving, the fresh gigs paying premiums, and levers to unleash your productivity without the personal-life crossover. We'll map the landscape shift, spotlight emerging opportunities with real transformations, unpack tools that turbocharge your day, and arm you with tactics to transition smoothly. For career changers, entrepreneurs, or climbers eyeing that next rung, this is your horizon scan: Roles not just in demand, but dialing up pay by 30% or more. Let's plot your course.

The Job Landscape Shift

The office isn't vanishing; it's upgrading. By 2025, AI's fingerprints are everywhere in professional realms, augmenting workflows rather than automating souls. Gartner's latest pulse? A whopping 45% productivity lift across sectors, as teams leverage models to sift data deluges and spark insights faster than solo sweat. It's not hype—it's happening: Finance pros now query natural-language dashboards for forecasts that once took days; engineers simulate prototypes in hours, not weeks.

This shift redefines roles at their core. The classic coder? Evolving into an AI orchestrator, less keyboard-bound and more conductor—prompting models like Grok-4 to generate boilerplate, then layering custom logic for bespoke brilliance. Marketers morph from ad sprayers to narrative navigators, using AI to A/B test at scale while they craft the emotional hooks that convert. Even HR? From resume sieves to talent alchemists, matching candidates via bias-checked algorithms that uncover hidden fits.

Why the seismic vibe? Demand's exploding—LinkedIn's 2025 Economic Graph shows AI-adjacent skills boosting hire rates by 40%, with premiums hitting 30% for hybrids like "prompt strategist." It's inclusive evolution: The educator in a underfunded district augments lesson plans; the solopreneur automates outreach to land dream clients. No one's left behind if you lean in—the landscape's tilting toward those who blend tech fluency with irreplaceable intuition. Your role? It's not obsolete; it's opportunity disguised as update.

Emerging Opportunities

If augmentation's the tide, opportunities are the surfs you catch—new gigs born from AI's wake, paying not just well, but wisely. We're talking roles that fuse your existing expertise with AI savvy, commanding salaries 30% above baselines: $150K+ for mid-level, scaling to $250K for leads. No gatekept by PhDs; accessible via upskilling bursts.

Spotlight the AI workflow designer: Architects of seamless automations, chaining tools like Zapier with LLMs to streamline ops—think a logistics whiz scripting bots that predict delays, saving firms millions. Or the AI content curator: Not ghostwriters, but refiners—feeding raw model outputs through human lenses for brand-aligned gold, hot in media where authenticity rules.

Then there's the ethics auditor: The rising star for diverse teams, stress-testing models for fairness in hiring or lending, with demand surging 60% post-2025 regs. Freelancers here pull $200/hour, consulting on everything from debiasing chatbots to equitable data sets.

To see the ripple, check this table of transformations—your before-and-after blueprint:

Traditional Role	AI-Evolved Gig	Pay Premium & Why It Pays	Entry Ramp
Teacher	Personalized Curriculum Curator	+35% ($85K avg.); Scales learning for diverse classrooms, boosting outcomes 25%.	Cert in edtech tools; pilot one class AI unit.
Marketer	AI Campaign Orchestrator	+30% ($140K); Hyper-targets with predictive analytics, ROI up 40%.	Build a sample funnel via no-code platforms.

AI SKILLS

Traditional Role	AI-Evolved Gig	Pay Premium & Why It Pays	Entry Ramp
Accountant	Financial Insight Forecaster	+28% ($130K); AI crunches numbers; you narrate strategic stories.	Master query tools like Tableau AI.
Nurse/Clinician	Patient Journey Optimizer	+32% ($110K); Triage bots free time for empathy-driven care.	Integrate wearables into shift protocols.

Traditional Role	AI-Evolved Gig	Pay Premium & Why It Pays	Entry Ramp
Sales Rep	Relationship AI Amplifier	+25% ($120K); Leads qualified by bots; closes with human rapport.	Script one AI-assisted pitch deck.

These aren't unicorns; they're your next profile tweak. A former client, Jamal from finance, jumped from ledger jockey to forecaster in six months—now remote, revenue-sharing gigs netting him freedom dividends. Emerging ops reward the versatile: Spot your lane, upskill, and surf.

Productivity Unleashed

Productivity in 2025 isn't about hustling harder—it's hacking smarter, with AI as your tireless deputy. Tools now don't just assist; they anticipate, turning "busy" into "breakthrough." The unlock? Delegating cognitive drudge so you amplify the high-touch: Strategy, synthesis, spark.

Take meetings: Otter.ai's evolved into a whisperer—real-time transcription, sentiment scans, and action-item auto-assigns that flag "Follow up on Q3 pivot—assign to Alex." No more frantic notes; post-call summaries hit your inbox, laced with highlights like "Key tension: Budget overruns—probe in next round." Teams using it report 30% faster follow-through, reclaiming hours for deep work.

Email? Superhuman or SaneBox AI triage inboxes like pros—prioritizing "Hot lead: Respond now" while drafting polite declines. I swapped my 2024 chaos for this; response times halved, focus tripled. For creators, Notion AI weaves research into outlines—prompt "Synthesize these 10 articles on sustainable branding," and it spits a scaffolded doc, ready for your voice.

Case in point: A mid-sized marketing firm I advised in Q2 2025. Campaign cycles? Dragged to 12 weeks with manual A/Bs and content spins. Enter AI levers: Jasper for variant gen, integrated with Google Analytics for real-time tweaks, and Canva's Magic Studio for visuals. Cycles slashed to six weeks—50% faster—while engagement lifted 22%. The team? Freed for client immersions, birthing bolder strategies like AR pop-ups that went viral. Burnout dipped; bonuses soared. It wasn't tech takeover; it was tandem triumph—the firm hit record Q4, crediting "human-AI harmony."

Rhetorical nudge: What's your bottleneck—research rabbit holes, repetitive reports? Tools like these (free tiers abound) aren't luxuries; they're levelers. Start with one: Integrate into your stack, measure the minutes saved, multiply by magic.

Transition Tactics

Shifting sands? Solid ground starts with self-audit: "AI-proof" your role by mapping must-keeps (empathy, ethics) against automatables (data entry, basic analysis). Prompt yourself: "What 20% of my tasks could AI handle tomorrow? What 20% only I can own?" Jot three swaps—e.g., bot for scheduling, you for storytelling. Then, prototype: Dedicate one hour weekly to a tool trial, logging ROI (time saved vs. learning curve). Network via LinkedIn's AI groups for peer pivots; aim for one coffee chat monthly.

For the leap, stack certs like Google's AI Essentials—quick, credible boosters. Track via a "Transition Tracker": Wins column for momentum, gaps for growth. It's iterative, not instant—my own 2023 hop took three audits, but unlocked that seven-figure flow.

Work transformed? Now, in Chapter 6, ground it in digital basics: Master prompt engineering to speak AI's language fluently.

Chapter 6:

Essential Digital Skills

You've glimpsed AI's work wizardry, but before you rev the engine on prompt-powered productivity, let's tune the chassis. This chapter's your pit stop for non-AI foundations—the digital fluency that turns "tech-curious" into "tech-capable." We're not diving into tools yet (that's next up); think bedrock basics like navigating the web like a pro or wrangling spreadsheets without sweat. Why? Because AI amplifies what's there—if your base wobbles, the whole build topples. We'll unpack why foundations matter, break down key skills with clear levels, roll up sleeves for hands-on drills, and cap with a quick readiness check. For the parent juggling tabs or the entrepreneur eyeing dashboards, this is your quiet confidence builder. Solid ground secured, then sky's the limit.

Why Foundations First

Hand someone a Ferrari without driver's ed, and what happens? Thrilling spinout—maybe a hedge-clipping detour, but zero destination. AI's that sports car: Sleek, supersonic, but it demands you grip the wheel with basics like throttle control (tech navigation) and blind-spot checks (data savvy). Skip the fundamentals, and you're not innovating—you're troubleshooting typos in prompts or fumbling file shares that kill momentum.

In 2025, this isn't theory; it's triage. Surveys from Deloitte's AI Readiness Index show a staggering 70% of AI initiatives flop not from fancy model glitches, but from yawning gaps in everyday digital chops—folks who can chat with Grok but freeze on a pivot table or public Wi-Fi risks. It's the hidden tax on hype: That consultant who nails ethics debates but can't secure a shared drive? Billable hours lost to leaks. Or the startup founder whose killer idea stalls because she Googles like it's 2010, missing the advanced filters that surface gold.

Foundations first flips this script. They're the unsexy scaffolding—boring until they're indispensable. In my early days, post-layoff scramble, I chased shiny LLMs while my Excel was kindergarten-level. Result? Hours wasted reformatting bot outputs. Once I backfilled basics—two weeks of drills—my experiments flew. It's empowerment 101: Master the mundane, and AI becomes your co-pilot, not a cranky rental. No gatekeeping here; these skills are free, fast, and yours to claim. Ready to lay the bricks?

Skill Breakdown

Digital foundations aren't a monolith; they're modular must-haves, each unlocking the next. We'll spotlight three pillars: Navigation (web mastery beyond basics), data basics (taming spreadsheets and files), and security (guarding your digital turf). No jargon—just actionable rungs to climb, from newbie to ninja.

Start with navigation: It's advanced search wizardry—operators like "site:edu AI ethics 2025" to laser in on credible hits, or Boolean combos ("prompt engineering" AND "beginner" -tutorial) to filter fluff. Why? In an info ocean, this saves hours, surfaces vetted sources for your AI experiments. Proficiency? Level 1: Basic Google (keywords only). Level 2: Operators in play (quotes for phrases). Level 3: Tools like Google Alerts for drip-fed updates on "AI job trends."

Data basics: Spreadsheets aren't sexy, but they're AI's best friend—Excel or Google Sheets for sorting, filtering, and charting trends. Think VLOOKUP to match client data, or pivot tables to summarize sales spikes. It's the bridge from raw numbers to insights AI can riff on. Levels: 1 (Enter data, simple sums). 2

(Formulas, basic charts). 3 (Macros for automation, conditional formatting for at-a-glance smarts).

Security rounds it out: Everyday armor like VPNs (e.g., ExpressVPN for public Wi-Fi shields) to encrypt traffic, password managers (LastPass) for breach-proof logins, and two-factor everywhere. In 2025's phishing frenzy, this prevents "oops" moments—like that rogue link nuking your freelance pitch. Levels: 1 (Strong passwords). 2 (2FA on key accounts). 3 (VPN habits, regular audits via Have I Been Pwned?).

To gauge your stack, here's a quick proficiency ladder:

- **Level 1:** Novice – Comfortable with email and social; dips into search but hits walls on organization.
- **Level 2:** Competent – Handles docs/spreadsheets for personal use; aware of risks but reactive (e.g., changes password post-breach).

- **Level 3:** Fluent – Navigates complex queries, builds data models, and proactively secures setups—like scripting VPN toggles.

These aren't silos; they synergize. Nail navigation to feed data basics with quality inputs, secured against snoops. In consulting, I've seen Level 3 folks outpace peers tenfold—because foundations free bandwidth for the fun stuff.

Hands-On Build

Theory's a map; drills are the miles. Building these skills isn't marathon marathons—it's weekly sprints, 30 minutes max, turning "I can't" into "I just did." The payoff? Momentum that snowballs, like compound interest for your digital IQ. Start where you stand, scale as you stick.

Week 1: Navigation bootcamp. Dedicate Tuesday to "Search Safari"—pick a topic like "2025 remote work hacks," then level up: Basic keywords first, then operators ("hacks" site:harvard.edu filetype:pdf).

Time it: 15 minutes hunting, 15 noting gems in a doc. By Friday, set a custom alert for weekly drops. I did this pre-Bali: Transformed scattershot scrolls into a curated feed, landing my first AI gig lead.

Week 2-3: Data deep dive. Wednesdays on spreadsheets—start with personal budgets in Excel: Column A for expenses, B for categories, then SUMIF formulas to tally "Dining Out" spends. Advance to pivots: Drag-drop to visualize monthly trends, add charts for "aha" visuals. Free resource? Microsoft's Garage tutorials—bite-sized videos. A novice client, Priya the edtech dreamer, hated numbers; after two weeks, she mapped student engagement data, spotting patterns that pitched her app to investors. From dread to dashboard pro.

Week 4: Security sprint. Thursdays for "Fortress Fridays"—install a VPN (test on café Wi-Fi), seed LastPass with 10 logins, enable 2FA on email/bank. Audit: Search your email for breaches, rotate any weak links. Make it stick with a habit hook, like VPN-on before coffee.

My 30-day anecdote? Early 2024, I was that overwhelmed dev—searches endless, sheets scrambled, security a shrug. Committed to these drills amid job hunts: Week 1 sharpened my resume research; Week 2 quantified freelance rates in pivots; Weeks 3-4 locked my portfolio site post-phish scare. By day 30? Landed a beta AI project, confidence cranked. It wasn't genius; it was grit—drills compounding into fluency. Yours? Pick one pillar per week, log in a "Skill Streak" journal. Miss a day? Restart, no shame. Hands-on isn't homework; it's your hidden accelerator.

Integration Check

Foundations fusing? Quick quiz: Rate your readiness 1-10 across the pillars—navigation (How fluid your searches?), data (Spreadsheet speed?), security

(Breach-proof basics?). Total under 20? Loop back to drills. 20+? You're primed.

Tally your score, celebrate the gaps closing. Skills solid? Now, in Chapter 7, deploy no-code productivity tools that build on this base for sweat-free wins.

Chapter 7:

AI Tools for Productivity

Ever stared at a blank project board, wondering if you'd need a dev degree to drag your ideas into reality? Spoiler: You don't. In 2025, no-code AI tools are the great equalizer—drag-and-drop dynamos that let you build automations, apps, and workflows without a single line of code. This chapter's your sweat-free intro to these efficiency engines, strictly task-focused: No artistic flourishes, just pure productivity firepower. We'll overview the ecosystem, deep-dive into writing and planning standouts with demos, weave them into seamless chains, and tweak for max output. For the busy consultant juggling gigs or the manager streamlining ops, this is your shortcut to "done" without the drain. By the end, you'll have a starter kit to automate the mundane—because who has time for busywork in the freedom chase?

Tool Ecosystem Overview

No-code AI isn't a single app; it's an ecosystem of interlocking powerhouses, categorized for your workflow woes. Think of it as a Swiss Army knife for tasks: Blades for writing (drafting reports, emails), planning (task boards, calendars), and beyond—data wrangling, form builders—all accessible via intuitive interfaces that hide the heavy lifting.

Writing tools lead the pack for content crunchers. Jasper's 2025 update? A beast—now with "context chaining," where it pulls from your uploaded docs to generate tailored briefs, slashing rewrite cycles by 40%. Pair it with Grammarly's AI overhaul, which not only polishes prose but predicts tone shifts for client comms.

Planning's domain shines with Notion AI and Airtable's smart bases. Notion's evolved into a mind-meld: Prompt "Outline Q4 goals from these notes," and it auto-populates databases with dependencies, deadlines, and Slack pings. Airtable? For ops pros, it's spreadsheets on steroids—AI formulas that auto-categorize entries, like tagging leads by engagement score without manual sorts.

Then there's the connectors: Zapier and Make.com as the glue, triggering actions across apps (e.g., new email to Trello card). Free tiers abound—Grok's no-code builder even lets you prototype simple bots via voice. The beauty? Scalable starts: Solo users kick off with basics; teams layer enterprise security. In my consultancy, swapping code for these cut setup from days to minutes—pure velocity. This ecosystem isn't overwhelming; it's your pick-and-plug path to frictionless flow.

Deep Dives

Zooming in: We'll demo writing and planning tools with nuts-and-bolts how-tos, starting with prompts that pack punch. These aren't vague vibes; they're templates tuned for task triumph—copy-paste ready, tweakable for your lane.

Writing first: Jasper's your report ranger. Sign up (free trial), upload a brief like "Q2 sales summary," then hit the 2025 "Chain Prompt" mode. Template: "Analyze [data file] for key metrics. Structure as: Executive summary (3 bullets), Trends (chart-ready), Action items (prioritized). Tone: Professional, concise." Boom—outputs a polished 800-worder in seconds, with embedded visuals. For emails? Swap to "Draft response to [client query], addressing [pain points], CTA: Schedule call." It nails nuance, like injecting urgency without pushiness. Pro tip: Feed it your style samples first for voice match—my drafts now sound like me, minus the typos.

Planning pivot: Notion AI's database dynamo. Create a page, type "/AI" to summon—template: "From [meeting notes], generate tasks with assignees, due dates, and progress trackers. Link to [Google Calendar]." It spins a kanban board, auto-flagging overlaps (e.g., "Conflict: Your 2 PM with team sync"). Airtable edges for data-heavy: Base setup, then "AI Field" for "Classify these entries by [criteria: urgency, source]." Instant smart lists—no formulas fumbled.

For at-a-glance picks, here's the showdown:

Tool	Cost (2025)	Key Features	Best For
Jasper	Free tier; $29/mo Pro	Context chaining, tone templates, export to Docs	Report drafting, email volleys
Grammarly AI	Free basic; $20/mo Premium	Predictive edits, plagiarism scans, style guides	Polishing pitches, compliance checks

Tool	Cost (2025)	Key Features	Best For
Notion AI	$10/mo add-on (free base)	Auto-task gen, database queries, integrations	Goal tracking, team wikis
Airtable	Free up to 1K records; $20/user/mo	AI sorting, formula builders, API hooks	Lead pipelines, inventory logs

These dives demystify: Start with one template, iterate outputs. In trials, users clock 35% faster task turnaround—your queue's new best friend.

Workflow Weaves

Tools solo are sharp; chained, they're unstoppable—automation tapestries that weave tasks into tapestries of time saved. Enter Zapier: The no-code conductor, linking apps with "Zaps" (if-this-then-that logic) that run on autopilot. No dev drudgery; just dropdowns and delays.

Basic weave: Email triage. Zap: Gmail "new high-priority" → Jasper draft response → Notion task log → Slack notify. Setup? 5 minutes: Authenticate apps, map fields (e.g., subject to prompt). Result: Inbox zero without the zen struggle.

Scale to ops: Freelancer flow—Google Form submission (client brief) → Airtable entry (AI-categorized) → Jasper outline gen → Email delivery. Add a delay for review; boom, end-to-end in under an hour.

Case spotlight: Take Lena, a freelance ops consultant I mentored in spring 2025. Swamped with 20 weekly client audits—manual data pulls, report spins, follow-ups eating weekends. We wove: Typeform intake → Zapier to Airtable (AI tags urgency) → Notion AI for summaries → Jasper for full decks → Auto-email via Gmail. Custom twist: Branch for "complex" flags, routing to her queue. Output? Doubled to 40 audits/month, revenue up 80% without burnout. "From frantic to focused," she said—weekends reclaimed for that novel outline (but that's Ch. 11's turf). Her secret? Test Zaps in sandbox mode first; tweak triggers quarterly.

These weaves aren't wizardry; they're wiring—start linear, layer loops. For the parent-preneur or team lead, it's the difference between drown and dominate: One chain, one chain reaction of reclaimed hours.

Optimization Tips

Max these tools? Customize ruthlessly: In Jasper, build a "swipe file" of winning prompts; Notion, script recurring AI queries via templates. Audit monthly—kill underused Zaps, A/B test outputs for sharper results. Pro hack: Layer free Grok for quick prototypes before premium commits. It's iterative polish: Tweak, track time saved, repeat.

Tasks tamed? Now, in Chapter 8, ground it deeper: Demystify data literacy for decisions that stick.

Chapter 8:

AI FOR CREATIVITY

What if your next sketch, stanza, or riff started not with a blank page, but a burst of "what ifs" from an unlikely muse? In 2025, AI isn't here to steal your thunder—it's the flint that sparks it, amplifying the wild, woolly chaos of human imagination. This chapter celebrates AI as your creative co-conspirator, purely for expression's sake: No pitches, no portfolios, just the joy of making. We'll explore how it ignites ideas without imitation, spotlight mediums like writing and music with spot-on tools, walk the iterative path from seed to symphony, and anchor it all in your unswappable voice. For the doodler in downtime, the lyricist in the shower, or the storyteller at heart, this is permission to play without pressure.

By the end, that inner artist? It'll feel less like a whisper, more like a roar—fueled, not faked.

AI as Creative Spark

Creativity's alchemy thrives on surprise, and AI's genius lies in the unexpected nudge—not cranking out carbon copies, but tossing curveballs that crack open your canon. Think of it as a brainstorming buddy who's read every book, heard every chord, but lacks your lived quirks: It ideates broadly, you infuse deeply. Midjourney v6, the 2025 visual virtuoso, exemplifies this—not a photo faker, but a dream weaver. Prompt "A forgotten library where books bloom into fireflies, cyberpunk dusk," and it births ethereal composites: Glowing shelves twisting into neon vines, evoking your grandma's attic fused with Blade Runner haze. The spark? That one image hooks a mood you couldn't name, launching a sketch series or mood board marathon.

It's not mimicry; it's multiplication. Tools like Grok's ideation mode riff associations—"If your poem's a rainy window, layer in echoes of jazz rain or quantum tears"—stretching your synapses without scripting the soul. In experiments, creators report 2x more "aha" moments, as AI handles the combinatorial grunt (mixing motifs from disparate eras) so you chase the emotional core. I've felt it: Staring at a blank canvas post-sunset walk, a quick prompt yields "Waves as whispered secrets in salt-sculpted code"—not the painting, but the portal to one. This isn't automation; it's acceleration, turning fleeting fancies into fertile ground. Your role? The selector, the shaper—the human heat that forges sparks into stars.

Medium Spotlights

AI spotlights mediums by spotlighting possibilities—enhancing writing's weave, music's melody, without overwriting your whimsy. Let's tune into two: Prose and sound, where tools act as sounding boards, not soloists.

Writing first: Sudowrite's 2025 "Plot Weaver" isn't a ghostwriter; it's a narrative navigator. Feed it a scene stub—"Eldritch fog rolls over the harbor, protagonist clutches a locket"—and it suggests branching paths: "The locket hums with ancestral voices, urging betrayal" or "It warms, revealing a map etched in starlight." You pick, remix, reject—building beats that surprise even you. For poets, its "Echo Engine" mirrors rhythms: Input your quatrain, get harmonic extensions that echo without echoing too loud. The result? Manuscripts that flow freer, drafts that dance.

Music's symphony? Suno 2025's harmony engine turns hums into hooks. Hum a melody line into your phone—"Wistful guitar riff over urban rain"—and it layers lush backings: Subtle synth swells or cello sighs that complement, not compete. Advanced mode? "Infuse with Balkan folk twists"—yielding a track that's yours at the bone, but broadened by global grooves you hadn't grooved to. No conservatory needed; just your voice (literal or lyrical) as the lead.

AI SKILLS

These aren't one-trick; they're versatile vaults. To unlock them, nail prompts with these best practices:

Specificity Sparks: Layer senses and stakes—"Not just 'forest scene,' but 'autumn crunch underfoot, hidden grief in the leaves.'"

Constraint Catalyzes: Limit outputs—"Three plot twists, under 50 words each"—to curate chaos.

Iteration Invitation: Always follow up—"Build on #2, but amp the irony"—for evolving echoes.

Mood Mapping: Prefix with vibe—"Melancholic indie folk, evoking lost summers"—to tune the tool's timbre.

Human Handover: End with "Now, your turn: Suggest my next line"—blurring lines beautifully.

Spotlit thus, AI doesn't dim your light; it diffuses it into dazzling spectra, inviting mediums to mingle in ways your solo mind might miss.

From Idea to Output

Creation's not a straight shot; it's a spiral—ideate, iterate, infuse—and AI smooths the loops without straightening the soul. Let's demo the dance: Start with a seed, say a hazy concept for a short story: "A clockmaker who winds time backward, chasing lost loves." Step one: Ideation burst. Prompt Midjourney or Grok: "Visualize a steampunk atelier where gears whisper regrets—mood board, five variants." Outputs flood: Brass dials dripping with dew-like tears, hourglasses blooming roses. Pick one that pangs—the gear-heart hybrid—and screenshot for reference.

Step two: Flesh the frame. Shift to Sudowrite: "Expand this image into a 200-word opening scene: Sensory details, internal monologue on fleeting fixes." It drafts: "His fingers, oil-stained sacraments, coax the escapement back—tick-tock inverting to tock-tick, a lover's laugh unspooling from the void." Solid scaffold; now iterate: "Revise for sharper sensory irony—clocks chime hollow in a room of full hearts."

Third pass: Your tweaks—"Swap laugh for a sigh's silk"—deepen the ache.

Music mirrors: Seed a Suno hum—"Plaintive violin over ticking percussion." First gen: A ballad skeleton. Iterate: "Layer ethereal vocals, fade to silence at 2:15 for emotional cliff." Output three: A haunting hybrid track, ready for lyrics you layer in GarageBand. The spiral? Each loop refines—AI proposes, you possess—turning vague vapor into vivid vessel.

My anecdote? Mid-2024, adrift in Bali's monsoons, I toyed with a poetry chapbook: "Threads of Tide and Time." Seed: Grok riffed titles from my scribbles—"Knots in the Current." Then Sudowrite wove drafts: One poem's "Waves knit scarves from shipwreck silk" hooked me. Iterations flew—ten versions, pruning purple prose, pinning personal pangs (a nod to my dad's faded letters). Midjourney visualized covers: Inky waves coiling into quills. Final output? A 40-page zine, printed on reclaimed paper—sold out at a beach pop-up, but the real win?

The ritual reignited my verse after years' drought. AI didn't author; it architected space for my story to breathe. Yours? Spiral freely— the output owns itself.

Authenticity Anchor

In this enhancer's embrace, remember: AI suggests symphonies, but your voice conducts. It's the timbre only you timbre—the scar's slant, the laugh's lilt—that anchors art to alive. Let tools trailblaze trails; you tread them true. Prompt as provocateur, not puppeteer—your edits are the essence.

Inspired? Now, in Chapter 9, ground those sparks in ethics: Build right, not just radiant.

Chapter 9:

AI and Online Business

Stepping into online business feels like planting a seed in digital soil—nurture it right, and it grows wild. But in 2025, AI's the sunlight and rain, accelerating without the army of hires. This chapter maps its supportive role in ventures from freelance gigs to e-com empires: Not the money math (that's next), but the muscle that lets solo operators punch like squads. We'll lay foundations for scaling sans sprawl, boost freelance and e-com with targeted lifts, streamline services into seamless streams, and outline launch essentials for grounded starts. For the side-hustler sketching Shopify stores or the creator dreaming digital products, this is your blueprint: AI as backbone, you as visionary. By the end, that venture won't just hum—it'll harmonize with your life.

Business AI Foundations

Online business thrives on leverage, and AI delivers it without the org chart bloat—scaling reach and responsiveness as if you cloned yourself, minus the identity crisis. At its core, it's about augmentation: Bots handle queries so you craft strategy; algorithms forecast trends so you focus on flavor. The ethos? Build lean, iterate fast, stay human.

Take chatbots for e-com: Tools like Gorgias or Intercom's AI in 2025 aren't scripted stiffs—they're conversational chameleons, trained on your brand voice to field "Does this tee run large?" with "Based on 500 reviews, size up for cozy—here's a style quiz to nail it." Result? Cart abandonment drops 25%, as shoppers feel seen, not shuttled. No round-the-clock team needed; one setup, infinite shifts.

Or personalization engines: Shopify's Magic now auto-tags customer vibes from past buys—"Eco-warrior? Curate sustainable swaps"—turning browsers into buyers without manual merchandizing marathons. It's scaling without scale: A solo jeweler I know went from 50 orders/month to 200, her AI concierge handling 80% of DMs while she sources gems in peace.

Foundations boil down to three: Integration ease (plug-and-play APIs), data dignity (anonymized insights only), and oversight loops (weekly AI audits for drift). In a world where 60% of online ventures fold from ops overload, this trio turns trickle to torrent—your business, boundless but bounded by your beat.

Freelance and E-Com Boosts

AI's freelance and e-com boosts aren't bells and whistles; they're the wind in your sails, propelling proposals and products with precision that feels prescient. For freelancers, it's the edge in crowded marketplaces—Upwork bids that land because they're laser-tuned, not lucky guesses.

Picture crafting proposals: Tools like Grok or Copy.ai in 2025 let you prompt "Tailor this Upwork pitch for a UX redesign gig: Highlight my Figma fluency, weave in client's pain from their site review [paste URL], end with a value-prop timeline." Output? A 300-word gem: "Your site's navigation maze? I've untangled similar for e-com clients, boosting conversions 35% via Figma prototypes—week 1 wireframes, week 4 live test." Personal, punchy, positioned—response rates spike 40% for users who AI-assist without over-relying. It's not cheating; it's channeling—your expertise, amplified.

E-com gets equal love: Inventory whispers from TradeGecko AI predict "Stock lavender soaps now—Mother's Day surge inbound"—averting sellouts or surpluses. Or customer journeys: Klaviyo's flows now AI-orchestrate "Abandoned cart? Nudge with a dynamic discount based on browse history." A dropshipper buddy automated this; her fulfillment fumbles fell 50%, letting her scout suppliers over coffee.

To niche it down, here's AI's play in key arenas:

Niche	AI Boost Example	Supportive Lift
Dropshipping	Inventory forecasters (e.g., Cin7 AI)	Auto-reorders based on trend signals; cuts overstock by 30%.
Freelance Writing	Proposal polishers (Copy.ai)	Custom bids from job specs; win rates up 35%.
Affiliate Marketing	Content calendars (Buffer AI)	Schedules posts timed to audience peaks; engagement +25%.

Niche	AI Boost Example	Supportive Lift
Handmade Crafts	Trend spotters (Etsy AI Insights)	Suggests "Vintage boho rising—stock macramé kits"; sales forecast accuracy 80%.
Consulting Services	Lead qualifiers (HubSpot AI)	Scores inquiries for fit; prioritizes hot ones, saving 10 hours/week.

These boosts democratize dynamism—freelancers from Manila to Miami level up, e-com hustles hum without heroics. Lean on AI for the lift; your intuition steers the ship.

Service Streamlining

Services—coaching, courses, consults—scale through systems, and AI streamlines them into silk-smooth offerings that feel bespoke, not baked. It's the invisible thread turning one-to-many into magic: Automate the assembly, personalize the delivery, iterate on autopilot.

Course builders lead: Teachable's AI in 2025 isn't a template tyrant; it's a curriculum curator. Upload your outline—"Module 1: Mindset shifts for solopreneurs"—and it generates quizzes, slides, even voiceover scripts in your timbre (via ElevenLabs integration). "Expand with three interactive polls on goal-setting pitfalls." Boom: A full module in minutes, laced with learner data hooks like "80% struggle with consistency—add a habit tracker embed." Creators report 50% faster launches, with completion rates up as AI adapts paths (e.g., "Struggling? Here's a micro-video detour").

Consulting? Calendly's AI now preps sessions: "Client's a fintech founder—pull their LinkedIn, suggest icebreakers on 2025 regs." Post-call, it transcripts and action-mines: "Key takeaway: Blockchain pivot—schedule follow-up in two weeks." No note scramble; just value velocity.

Case in the wild: Raj, a solo graphic designer turned agency phantom in late 2024. Overwhelmed by custom requests—mood boards, revisions, client chats—he wove AI: Canva Magic for initial mocks ("Brand: Minimalist tech—generate five logo variants from color palette"), then Descript for client recaps ("Edit this call for highlights, email summary"). Streamlined? His service went from bespoke one-offs to a "Design Accelerator" package—AI-generated starters he refined, scaling to 15 clients/month without burnout. From lone wolf to virtual firm: "It cloned my process, not my passion," he shared over a virtual toast. Now, he mentors via AI-assisted group cohorts, his original spark undimmed.

Streamlining isn't shrinkage; it's expansion—services that serve more, stress less. Prototype one flow this week; watch the weave tighten.

Launch Essentials

Launching lean? Validate with AI-fueled steps: First, audience echo—prompt Grok "Survey 10 questions for [niche] pain points," poll via Typeform, analyze responses for "must-solves." Second, MVP mock: Use Figma AI to wireframe your offer, test with a beta circle for feedback loops. Third, traction test: Run a micro-campaign—AI-optimized ad copy on LinkedIn, track clicks to conversions. Iterate thrice before go-live; it's proof over polish.

Business built? Now, in Chapter 10, cash in: Monetize those skills for streams that sustain.

Chapter 10:

EARNING WITH AI SKILLS

You've built the skills, woven the workflows, and glimpsed the creative fire—now, the real thrill: Turning that toolkit into treasure. In 2025's AI gold rush, earning isn't about grinding harder; it's leveraging smarter, where a well-prompted project pays like a full week's legacy work. This chapter's your opportunity atlas: Pure pathways to income, no moral mazes yet. We'll survey the monetization landscape with its sky-high ceilings, explore freelance and agency routes with a skill-to-cash map, unpack scaling secrets like portfolios and pricing, and measure success through freedom lenses. For the career pivot eyeing $5K months or the entrepreneur plotting passive streams, this is your ignition. By the end, earning won't feel elusive—it'll feel engineered, one strategic step at a time.

Monetization Landscape

The 2025 AI economy isn't a bubble; it's a boomtown, with freelancers and founders cashing in on skills that were sci-fi a decade ago. Picture this: Consultants commanding $200/hour for prompt audits that slash client ops by 40%, or no-code builders flipping custom automations for $10K pops. Platforms like Upwork report AI gigs up 300% year-over-year, with median rates hitting $75/hour—30% above general freelance averages. Why the surge? Demand's insatiable: SMBs crave AI edges without in-house hires, while enterprises hunt ethicists and integrators to navigate regs like the EU AI Act.

It's not just hourly hustle; passive plays proliferate. Digital products—AI-curated templates, chat agents for niches like real estate—sell on Gumroad for $47 a pop, scaling to $20K/month with zero marginal cost. Affiliate streams? Promote tools like Jasper via newsletters, earning 20% recurring on $50K referrals. And the crown jewel: Equity in AI startups, where a workflow wizard consults for shares that vest into six figures.

This landscape levels the field: No Ivy pedigree required—just demonstrable chops. In my seven-figure consultancy arc, it started with $500 prompt gigs; now, retainers roll in at $15K/month. The highs? Limitless, if you ladder up: Entry at $50/hour, mastery at $300+. But it's choice-rich: Gig economy for flexibility, product empires for sovereignty. Your slice? It's waiting—claim it with the pathways ahead.

Pathways Explored

Monetization's menu is vast, but two entrees dominate for AI aces: Freelance for fast entry and agencies for amplified reach. Freelance is the solo sprint—platforms like Fiverr or Contra let you list "AI workflow optimizer" at $97 starters, scaling to $2K packages as reviews stack. Target niches: E-com owners needing chatbots, marketers craving content chains. The flow? Profile polish (AI-draft your bio), gig gallery (case studies from Ch. 7 weaves), and outreach blitz—cold DMs via LinkedIn AI-curated lists, landing 20% response.

Agencies flip the script: Bundle your skills into boutique firms, like "Prompt Partners" for brand voice tuning. Start micro: Subcontract under established shops, then spin solo with white-label tools (e.g., Zapier agencies charging $5K setups). Or virtual collectives—Discord crews where you lead AI ethics modules for $1K/session groups. The edge? Recurring revenue: Monthly retainers for model maintenance, turning one-off fixes into $3K/month lifelines.

Both paths flex: Freelance for nomad vibes (Bali billing), agencies for network nets (referrals galore). To map your match, here's a skill-to-income blueprint:

1. **Prompt Engineering:** $80-150/hr freelance (Upwork bots); $4K/month agency retainers for e-com personalization.

2. **No-Code Builds:** $1-5K per app (Fiverr prototypes); $10K+ agency packages for CRM overhauls.

3. **Data Literacy:** $100/hr audits (Contra insights); $2K workshops via agency cohorts for SMB analytics.

4. **Workflow Automation:** $500-2K gigs (Contra chains); $15K quarterly agency contracts for ops scaling.

5. **Creative Amplification:** $75/hr content curation (Fiverr hybrids); $3K/month agency subscriptions for ad creatives.

These aren't hypotheticals—pathways paved by peers like the ex-teacher now freelancing ed-AI tutors at $120/hour, or the marketer's micro-agency hitting $50K quarters. Pick your pace: Dive freelance for proof, agency for power. Either way, it's your skills, syndicated.

Scaling Secrets

Earning starts small, but scaling's the sorcery—turning $1K gigs into $100K arcs through portfolios that pop and pricing that persuades. First, portfolio power: It's your silent salesperson, not a static PDF but a living showcase. Build on Notion or Carrd: Embed before-afters (e.g., "Pre-AI: 10-hour report; Post: 2-hour gem with 3x insights"), video testimonials, and interactive demos (Grok-powered "Try my prompt here"). Update quarterly—add metrics like "Saved client $20K in ops"—to magnetize higher tiers. In 2025, 70% of hires scan portfolios first; make yours a conversion machine.

Pricing's the pivot: Ditch hourly traps for value vaults. Tier it: Bronze ($497 one-off audits), Silver ($1,997 packages with tweaks), Gold ($4,997/month retainers + exclusives). Anchor high—start quotes 20% above target, negotiate down for perceived wins. Test via A/B: "Fixed pricing" vs. "Custom consult"—the latter nets 15% more. Bundle upsells:

Core service + "AI maintenance add-on" for 30% revenue bump.

Case in motion: Meet Tara, the 2024 side-hustler moonlighting AI content tweaks for bloggers—$300 gigs, sporadic. Scaling secret one: Portfolio pivot. She curated a "Content Cascade" site: Case studies with swipe files (prompts that 2x'd engagement), pulling in inbound leads. Secret two: Tiered pricing—launched a $97/month "Prompt Club" for templates, scaling to 100 members ($9K passive). By mid-2025? Agency lite: Partnered with three freelancers for overflow, hitting $100K YTD without full-time tilt. "From feast-or-famine to flow," she messaged—weekends still hers, revenue recurring. Her hack? Quarterly "value audits": Survey clients, refine offerings (e.g., add voice-mode integrations). It's not luck; it's levers—pull them, watch the lift.

Scale isn't sprawl; it's smart stacking. Prototype your portfolio this week; price one offer boldly. The secrets? They compound, carrying you from side spark to sustained blaze.

Freedom Metrics

Earning's endgame isn't endless zeros—it's equilibrium, tracked via time-vs-revenue dashboards. Simple setup: Google Sheets with columns for "Gig Value," "Hours Invested," "Freedom Quotient" (revenue/hour + non-billable joy hours). Aim for $100+/hour thresholds; flag dips below 80% for tweaks (e.g., automate low-ROI tasks). Monthly review: "Did this $5K win reclaim a week, or just fill it?" It's the north star—monetization measured by margin, not just money.

Earning unlocked? Now, in Chapter 11, wield it ethically: Foundations to build right, not just rich.

Chapter 11:

ETHICAL USE OF AI

Ethics in AI isn't a sidebar—it's the spine that keeps your work standing tall. As we pivot from earnings to embedding values, this chapter drills into responsible usage: Your daily guardrails for wielding tools with integrity, sans the broader societal sermons or classroom vibes. We're talking personal responsibilities that sharpen your edge, from sniffing out biases to owning transparency. We'll unpack why ethics builds unbreakable trust (with 2025's hard lessons), tackle bias detection with practical tools, put values into play with real examples, and craft your personal code to make it stick. For the freelancer fine-tuning prompts or the creator curating outputs, this is your compass: Use AI right, and it elevates not just your game, but your good name. By the end, ethics won't feel like a chore—it'll feel like your quiet superpower.

Ethics as Edge

In a world where AI's shine can blind, ethics is the polish that makes it gleam—for you. It's not virtue-signaling; it's value-adding, the differentiator that turns "good enough" gigs into "go-to" status. Clients don't just want results; they want reliability—proof you're not cutting corners that could crater their rep. When you bake in responsibility, trust compounds: Referrals roll in, rates rise, and you sleep sounder knowing your work withstands scrutiny.

2025's scandals hammer this home. Remember the "Echo Ad Debacle"? A major beauty brand's AI campaign, meant to celebrate diversity, spat out hyper-filtered faces that erased ethnic textures—sparking boycotts and a $50 million class-action suit. Or the fintech fiasco where loan algorithms, unchecked for fairness, denied approvals along invisible zip-code lines, fueling regulatory crackdowns. These weren't villain plots; they were rushed rollouts, blind to blind spots. The fallout? Brands hemorrhaged loyalty—Nielsen clocked a 25% trust dip in AI-driven marketing post-incidents—while ethical peers surged: Firms with transparency audits saw client acquisition jump 40%.

Your edge? Ethics as moat. In consulting, I've pitched "bias-vetted integrations" over bare-bones builds—winning bids because buyers bet on bulletproof. It's proactive armor: Spot issues early, solve them swiftly, and position as the steward who safeguards. In an era of easy audits (one viral tweet away from exposure), this isn't optional—it's oxygen. Lean into it, and AI doesn't just work for you; it works with your word.

Bias and Fairness

Bias sneaks in like fog—subtle, pervasive, skewing outputs before you blink. It's not malice; it's math mirroring messy data, amplifying inequities if unchecked. Your responsibility? Vigilance in usage: Probe prompts, vet datasets, deploy detectors to ensure fairness flows through every layer. In 2025, tools make this muscle memory—free, fast, and foolproof for solo ops.

Start with detection dynamos: Hugging Face's Bias Probe scans models mid-prompt—"Run this hiring sim: Does it favor Ivy Leaguers?"—flagging disparities with heatmaps (e.g., 30% lower scores for non-traditional paths). Or Perspective API from Google: Paste ad copy, get toxicity scores on stereotypes, tweaking "ambitious leader" to neutral "driven innovator" if flags wave. For visuals, Midjourney's Fairness Filter (v6 add-on) audits generations: "This diverse team render? 80% balanced representation—good to go."

Fairness extends to feedback loops: Post-deploy, log user interactions—"Did this rec engine overlook underrepresented creators?"—and retrain iteratively. No PhD needed; these are browser-based, with dashboards that dashboard your diligence.

To checkpoint your process, here's a scannable Ethical Checkpoints table—run it pre-launch:

Checkpoint	What to Do	Red Flag Example	Fix Fast
Prompt Parity	Test variations for demographic neutrality (e.g., gender swaps).	"Nurse" defaults female in outputs.	Add explicit diversity cues: "Inclusive roles across genders."
Data Diversity	Audit sources for balance (age, region, etc.).	Training set 70% urban U.S.—rural blind spots.	Supplement with global datasets via Kaggle.

Checkpoint	What to Do	Red Flag Example	Fix Fast
Output Audit	Score for equity (tools like Fairlearn).	Job recs skew 60% to one ethnicity.	Retrain with debiasing scripts—rerun till <5% variance.
User Impact	Simulate end-user views (diverse beta tests).	Accessibility gaps for non-English speakers.	Integrate multilingual checks; loop in feedback.
Transparency Tag	Disclose AI involvement upfront.	Hidden edits erode trust in reports.	Watermark outputs: "AI-assisted, human-vetted."

These aren't hurdles; they're habits—5 minutes per checkpoint, compounding to campaigns that convert without controversy. In my practice, a quick bias probe saved a client's wellness app from wellness-washing—fair recs boosted retention 20%. Fairness isn't finish line; it's foundation—build on it, watch your work withstand winds.

Values in Action

Ethics leaps from list to life when values drive decisions—transparency as your North Star, turning "what works" into "what's worthy." It's usage in the trenches: Label AI's hand clearly, invite audits openly, iterate inclusively. Examples abound: In content creation, watermark generations—"Powered by Grok, refined by me"—so audiences appreciate the hybrid without haze. For workflows, dashboard disclosures: "This forecast uses anonymized data; query for sources." It's not overkill; it's ownership, fostering feedback that fuels better builds.

Deeper: Consent in chains. When automating client outreach, prompt for opt-ins—"Verify preferences before send"—averting spam shadows. Or in creative collabs, credit the code: "Built on open-source Llama, customized for vibe." These actions aren't abstract; they anchor alliances, as seen in 2025's "Trust Transparency Index," where open ops correlated with 35% higher loyalty scores.

Anecdote from the frontlines: Early 2025, I greenlit a campaign for a fitness brand—AI-generated ads targeting "motivated millennials." Initial outputs? Glossy gym gods, all lithe and light-skinned, ignoring the diverse data dump I'd fed. Bias alert—mirroring stock photo pitfalls, alienating broader bodies. Pause, probe: Fairlearn flagged 45% underrep for plus-size and POC queries. Values in action: I rallied the team for a transparency huddle—"Here's the glitch; let's gut-check together." Revised prompts: "Diverse athletes in real motion, all sizes celebrated." Rerun, review: Balanced visuals that breathed authenticity—curvy climbers, elder yogis, joyful jams. Launch? Not just clicks—community cheers, with UGC flooding in. The brand? Retained me for quarterly ethics embeds, turning a near-miss into a mandate. That revision wasn't rework; it was redemption—values vivifying the vision, from biased blip to inclusive beacon.

Action it: Next project, script one transparency touch (e.g., "AI role: Idea gen; my role: Soul stitch"). It's the ripple that radiates—your work, woven with worth.

Personal Code

Craft your code like a prompt: Concise, core, yours. Here's a template oath—adapt, affirm, act:

"I commit to AI use that honors humanity: Probe for bias before proceed; disclose assists transparently; prioritize fairness in every fork; iterate with impact in mind. When in doubt, default to do-good—because tools serve, but integrity endures."

Pin it—desk note, bio badge. Review quarterly: "Lived it? Lived up?" It's your ethical engine, idling for ignition.

Ethics embedded? Now, in Chapter 12, enhance learning: Loops that keep you lifelong sharp.

Chapter 12:

AI AND EDUCATION

Education's always been a spark—igniting minds, reshaping futures—but in 2025, AI's the accelerant, turning one-size-fits-all lessons into tailored torches. This chapter silos into learning and teaching aids, no healthcare detours: Purely the classroom and beyond, where AI personalizes paths without prescribing them. We'll pivot through education's big shift toward bespoke brains, spotlight learner tools like smart flashcards for solo scholars, amplify teachers with grading ghosts and integrations, and push on equity to ensure no one's left in the lecture hall shadows. For the adult reskiller cramming code after kids' bedtime or the educator eyeing efficiency without losing the human hum, this is your upgrade. By the end, AI won't feel like a gadget—it's the gentle guide making smarter selves, one adaptive nudge at a time.

Education's AI Pivot

Remember cramming for finals with a textbook that droned on, ignoring your midnight epiphanies? 2025 flips that script: AI's pivot is personalization at planetary scale, where learning bends to you, not the other way. It's the boom of adaptive platforms that diagnose drifts and deploy detours—market exploding from $1.72 billion this year to over $5 billion by decade's end, per industry pulses. No more marching in lockstep; algorithms map your mastery gaps, serving bites that stick.

Duolingo's the poster child: Their 2025 rollout of 148 AI-forged courses isn't rote repetition—it's role-play realms, where your flubs feed back into storylines that evolve. Stumble on subjunctives? The app spins a "what-if" tale with gentle grammar ghosts, boosting retention 40% via that 51% user surge they clocked on AI-first tweaks. It's not babysitting; it's bespoke bootcamp—adjusting pace for the harried parent (five-minute vocab vines) or the immersion junkie (convo sims with virtual Parisians).

This pivot ripples wider: Khan Academy's AI now curates "knowledge webs," linking algebra to your astronomy hobby for contextual clicks. Or Coursera's adaptive audits, rerouting dropouts with micro-modules that match mood (video for visuals, quizzes for kinesthetics). The ethos? Equity in efficiency—learners log 25% more hours when paths feel personal, not punitive. In my workshops, I've seen skeptics soften: "It's like a tutor who never tires, but knows when to tease." Education's not evolving—it's empathizing, one data-driven detour at a time.

Learner Tools

For learners—especially us adults reskilling amid 9-to-5s—AI tools are the midnight mentors, distilling oceans into sips that sink in. Flashcard AIs lead the charge: No more rote rote; these dynamos space repetitions like a memory whisperer, predicting plateaus and popping prompts just before you forget. Anki's 2025 glow-up? AI-curated decks that pull from your notes—"From this Python snippet, generate cloze tests on loops"—yielding adaptive stacks that evolve with errors, slashing study time 30% for busy bees.

Quizlet's Magic Mode takes it social: Upload a syllabus, get gamified flashcards with AI-generated mnemonics ("Loops? Picture a hamster wheel of hilarity"). Pair with voice drills for commuters—prompt "Quiz me on APIs while I drive"—and it's commute-to-competence. For deeper dives, Memrise's neural nets now remix user content: "Blend these bio terms with pop culture hooks"—turning mitosis into Marvel metaphors.

Case in the clutch: Enter Lena, 42, a marketing vet pivoting to data science post-layoff. 2024's her haze—endless Udemy scrolls, zero stick. Enter AI aids: She starts with Coursebox's reskilling rig, which scans her resume and spits a "Data Dash" path—flashcards via Brisk AI for SQL syntax, spaced to her 20-minute lunch slots. "It knew I bombed joins twice—next deck? Visual venns with coffee-break quizzes." By month three, DARPA-inspired tools (echoing their adult AI reboot) layer in STEM sims: Grok-powered "What-if" scenarios, like "Debug this dataset glitch in a virtual lab." Outcome? Certified in six months, landing a $95K analyst gig—her journey? "From flashcards to flow state; AI didn't teach—it tuned me to learn." For reskillers like her (and the 60% workforce eyeing upskills by 2030), these tools aren't crutches—they're catapults, turning "too late" into "just in time."

Teacher Amplifiers

Teachers: You're the alchemists, but admin alchemy steals the magic—enter AI amplifiers, the sidekicks slashing stacks so you sparkle. Grading bots top the triage: Gradescope's 2025 suite doesn't just score; it scaffolds—AI parses essays for rubric riffs ("Strong thesis, but evidence echo thin—suggest peer pair?"), cutting feedback loops from hours to minutes. Rubrics auto-adapt too: "For this diverse class, flag cultural biases in responses." Result? 40% more time for those hallway heart-to-hearts.

Brisk Teaching weaves it wider: Chrome-extended, it zaps lesson plans from standards—"Generate a 7th-grade civics unit on voting rights, with AI polls for engagement"—then integrates quizzes that self-grade on the fly. MagicSchool.ai? The oracle for overload: "Differentiate this math module for ELLs"—outputs tiered tasks, from visual vids to voice-guided solves.

These aren't replacements; they're releasers—frees you to orchestrate the unscripted, like debate detours that ignite. To plug them in, here's a bullet blitz of classroom integrations, tuned for 2025's hybrid hum:

Lesson Launcher: Canva Magic Studio—AI-draft slides from scribbles ("Theme: Ecosystems, vibe:

Interactive"), embed AR explorations for hands-on without hassle.

Engagement Engine: Kahoot!'s AI host—auto-generates quizzes from texts, adapts difficulty mid-game ("Class avg 70%? Pivot to teams"), spiking participation 35%.

Feedback Forge: Turnitin's Insight—beyond plagiarism, AI spots skill gaps ("Synthesis weak across board—recommend group mind-maps"), with equity audits for fair flags.

Collab Catalyst: Google Classroom's Gemini boost—AI-summarizes discussions ("Key themes: Climate action"), suggests extensions like "Link to local policy sim."

Accessibility Ally: Microsoft Copilot for Education—real-time captions/translations in lessons, plus "Simplify this para for dyslexia-friendly flow."

In my edtech consults, a high-school history prof swapped weekend war stories for AI-graded primaries—reclaimed hours for field trips that flipped textbooks alive. Amplifiers don't dim your dim; they dial up the dazzle, letting pedagogy breathe.

Equity Push

AI's education pivot shines brightest when it bridges, not builds, divides—2025's access initiatives are the equity engines, democratizing tools for under-resourced realms. Khan Academy's free AI tutors now offline-capable, beaming adaptive paths to rural routers; Duolingo's low-data modes serve 100M+ in low-bandwidth zones. Initiatives like UNESCO's AI4Equity fund open-source graders for global classrooms, while platforms like Disco's upskilling hubs offer subsidized reskilling for gig workers. The push? Universal access—closing the 20% digital divide gap, one localized lesson at a time. It's not charity; it's the core—smarter for all, or stalled for some.

Smarter selves? Now, in Chapter 13, broader impacts: Networking in the neural age.

Chapter 13:

AI in Healthcare and Society

AI's tendrils stretch far beyond screens into the sinews of society, reshaping how we heal and how we hold each other up. This chapter peers into those ripples, with a sharp focus on healthcare's horizons—no detours into job futures, just the human heartbeat of progress and its pains. We'll horizon-scan diagnostics' dazzling diagnostics, weave safety nets with predictive prowess, confront equity's thorny challenges in underserved corners, and rally with a collective call to advocate. For the parent tracking family vitals or the community builder eyeing better bonds, this is the societal stitch: AI as amplifier of care, not cure-all. By the end, you'll see not just tech's tide, but how to steer it toward shores that lift all boats.

Healthcare Horizons

Healthcare in 2025 isn't a waiting room marathon; it's a marathon with AI as your pacing coach, sprinting diagnostics from hunch to hyper-precise. The horizon gleams with tools that sift symptoms like seasoned sleuths, catching curves no clinic clock could clock. At the vanguard? IBM Watson Health's evolutions, now a neural navigator fusing multimodal data—scans, labs, histories—into insights that shave weeks off workflows.

Watson's 2025 leap? "Discovery Engine 2.0," an AI that doesn't just flag anomalies; it forecasts forks. Feed it a chest X-ray, and it doesn't stop at "possible pneumonia"—it layers in genomic snippets and lifestyle logs to predict "80% sepsis risk if untreated; recommend targeted antivirals." Accuracy? Clocking

95% in trials, up from 2024's 88%, thanks to self-healing agents that debug on the fly, adapting to new variants like flu strains mid-season. Imaging's the star: Watson's orchestration now integrates with hospital PACS, auto-prioritizing urgent ultrasounds—cutting radiologist wait times 60%, freeing them for complex calls.

This isn't isolated wizardry; it's woven wide. PathAI's slide scanners pair with Watson for biopsy blitzes, spotting cancers 30% earlier in low-resource labs. Or wearable tie-ins: Fitbit's AI pulses to Watson clouds, alerting "Atrial fib spike—tele-echo now?" The ripple? Lives lengthened, not just logged—global trials show 20% faster interventions, turning "wait and see" into "see and save." Horizons like these aren't distant dawns; they're today's toolkit, democratizing detection for docs and patients alike. Your scan tomorrow? Smarter, swifter, because AI's rewriting the rules of remedy.

Safety and Social Nets

Safety in society's fabric frays fast without nets, and AI's 2025 weave is predictive alerts—the vigilant threads that snag slips before they snag souls. These aren't reactive buzzers; they're proactive prophets, sifting signals from streams of data to safeguard the vulnerable. In healthcare, it's the early whisper: "This vitals dip? Sepsis shadow—alert ER now." Tools like Epic's AI now embed in EHRs, scanning for subtle shifts—heart rate wobbles in elders, med non-adherence in chronic cases—flagging 40% more at-risks before crises crest.

Social nets stretch further: Community health platforms like Color Health's AI forecast outbreaks in neighborhoods, texting "Flu surge nearby—vax pop-up tomorrow?" for low-income zip codes. Or mental health monitors: Crisis Text Line's bots parse patterns in pleas, escalating "high despair" to counselors 25% faster. The magic? Multimodal mesh—wearables, claims, even social feeds—yielding alerts that adapt: "Mom's isolation score up? Suggest peer circle link."

But nets need nuance; unchecked, they snag the wrong souls. Privacy protocols now standard—federated learning keeps data local—yet the win is in weave: 2025 pilots show 35% drop in ER revisits via these sentinels. For society, it's the buffer: Not Big Brother, but big brother—watching wings so we don't clip them.

To map the mesh, here's a table of key impact areas, spotlighting how predictive alerts fortify:

Impact Area	AI Alert Example	Safety Net Lift
Chronic Care	Wearable flags insulin dips pre-hypo.	30% fewer hospitalizations; empowers self-management for diabetics.

Impact Area	AI Alert Example	Safety Net Lift
Elderly Oversight	Home sensors predict falls from gait glitches.	Alerts kin/caregivers—reduces isolation incidents 25%.
Mental Health	Chat logs spot escalation in therapy texts.	Routes to hotlines; cuts suicide risks 20% in trials.
Community Outbreaks	Geo-data predicts spread in underserved blocks.	Targeted testing—lowers transmission 15% in pilots.
Post-Op Recovery	App monitors wound healing via photo AI.	Early infection pings docs—slashes readmits 40%.

These areas aren't silos; they're society's sinew—alerts that alert us to care more deeply, netting falls before they fracture.

Equity Challenges

AI's healthcare horizons dazzle, but equity's the eclipse—underserved access casting long shadows where rural clinics creak under connectivity crags and data deserts. In 2025, the divide digs deeper: Urban hubs hum with Watson weaves, while rural realms ration bandwidth, leaving 20 million Americans—mostly in flyover fringes—beyond the AI arc. Challenges? Algorithmic blind spots baked from biased benchmarks (90% urban-sourced), plus infrastructure ills: Spotty 5G starves tele-diagnostics, and low-lit litacies lock out low-income learners from app interfaces.

Underserved souls suffer silent: Black and Indigenous patients face 15% higher misdiagnosis rates from models mirroring majority meds, while rural elders wait weeks for scans that city slickers snag same-day.

Funding fumbles compound—safety-net providers snag just 10% of AI grants, per 2025 audits—leaving clinics to cobble clunky chatbots that glitch on accents or dialects.

Yet sparks flicker: Initiatives like HRSA's Rural AI Fund seed $500M for offline-capable tools, bridging bytes to backroads. Telemedicine titans—Teladoc's low-data modes—now serve 70% more remote reaches, with voice-AI triaging in 200+ tongues.

Case carved from clay: The Willow Creek Clinic in Montana's badlands, a 2024 holdout with one doc for 5,000 souls. Challenges crushed: No broadband for Watson, staff stretched thin on seasonal swells. Enter a 2025 pilot via Episcopal Health Foundation's AI4Rural: Drone-delivered diagnostics kits with edge-AI—solar-powered scanners that process X-rays onsite, beaming summaries via satellite bursts. Predictive alerts ping "TB trace in teen cohort—quarantine quiz"—catching clusters clinics missed. Equity edge? Culturally tuned prompts

(Navajo nods in nutrition nudges), slashing no-shows 40%. Transformation? From triage triage to proactive patrols: Patient portals via SMS for elders sans smartphones, outcomes up 25%—fewer ER airlifts, more local lives mended. Willow's doc? "AI didn't replace us; it reached us—now we reach them." It's proof: Challenges conquered not by cash alone, but co-design—rural voices in the code, turning access deserts to oases.

Equity's not endpoint; it's the ethic—press for it, and AI heals holistically.

Collective Call

Society's strengthened when we advocate as chorus: Join the call—sign petitions for inclusive datasets (e.g., White House AI Equity Pledge), volunteer beta tests for rural rigs, or amplify voices via #HealthAIForAll threads. Prompt for yourself: "What one underserved story can I share to spotlight the gap?" It's the nudge that nets change—your voice, the vital sign.

Society strengthened? Now, in Chapter 14, prep for job waves: Lifelong loops that keep you ahead.

Chapter 14:

AUTOMATION AND THE FUTURE OF JOBS

Automation's hum isn't a harbinger—it's a herald, signaling shifts where machines muscle the mundane so humans master the meaningful. In December 2025, as we stand mid-decade, this chapter forecasts those tides: Strategic prep for reskilling amid resurgences, no pep talks, just precise pivots. We'll ground in automation's dual-edged realities with fresh WEF data, forecast field-by-field with safest harbors highlighted, map proactive pivots via certs and cases, and lens it through opportunity's unyielding gaze. For the strategist scanning horizons or the mid-lifer plotting portfolios, this is your tactical terrain: Not fear of the flux, but fluency in its flow. By the end, the future won't loom—it's a ledger you lead.

Automation Realities

2025 marks automation's inflection: Not wholesale wipeouts, but targeted takeovers where bots bite into rote roles, birthing hybrids that demand human oversight. The World Economic Forum's Future of Jobs Report 2025 lays it bare: By 2030, technological disruption will reshape 22% of global jobs, displacing 92 million positions in declining sectors like data entry and basic assembly, while creating 170 million new ones—netting a 78 million opportunity surge. That's no apocalypse; it's augmentation at scale, with AI and robotics as the prime movers, outpacing green transitions or geopolitical shakes.

Displacements hit hardest in administrative trenches—think clerks automated by RPA (robotic process automation) tools that now handle 70% of invoice workflows without a glitch. Yet creations cluster in emergent edges: AI trainers, sustainability analysts, and digital trust specialists, roles blending tech with touch that machines mimic but can't master.

Slower economic growth tempers the tide, projecting 1.6 million net losses from inflation drags, but macro trends like the green pivot add counterbalances—EV assembly lines birthing 2 million skilled retrofits by decade's close.

This reality isn't random; it's reskilling's runway. WEF clocks 40% of core skills evolving by 2027, urging strategic stockpiles: Not hoarding yesterday's hacks, but hedging with hybrid fluency. In boardrooms I've briefed, the pivot's clear—firms investing 10% of payroll in upskilling see 25% less churn. Automation's truth? It displaces drudgery, demands direction—your prep now plots the plenty.

Field-by-Field Forecasts

Forecasts fragment by field, with creative realms as resilient reefs—human ingenuity's last stand against algorithmic tides. By 2030, WEF projects creative industries (arts, design, media) facing just 12% disruption, safest harbor as empathy and originality outpace outputs. Coders? 28% shift—routine scripting succumbs to no-code, but architect roles explode 35% for system symphonists. Healthcare? Diagnostics dip 15% to bots, but care coordination surges 40%, valuing the relational read no scan supplies.

Finance flips faster: 32% of teller tasks automated, birthing fintech ethicists at 25% growth. Manufacturing? Assembly lines lose 20 million slots to cobots, offset by 30 million in predictive maintenance pros. Education endures: Tutoring tech trims 18%, but curriculum curators climb 22%, weaving AI into wisdom. Retail? Checkout clerks fade 25%, but experience engineers rise 28%—think VR stylists in virtual aisles.

These aren't dooms; they're directions—fields fracturing into "augment or atrophy." Creatives thrive on the uncodifiable: A novelist's nuance, a designer's daring. To navigate, here's reskill roadmaps, tailored per terrain:

Creative Fields: Layer intuition with tools—Midjourney mastery (3-month Coursera track); pivot to "AI art director" gigs, blending prompts with palettes for 20% premium pay.

Tech/Engineering: From code to orchestrate—Google's Machine Learning Crash Course (free, 15 hours); target "hybrid dev" certs, upskilling syntax to strategy in 6 weeks.

Healthcare: Diagnostics to dynamics—edX's AI in Health (4 weeks); reskill in "patient navigator" paths, fusing empathy with Epic AI for 15% role resilience.

Finance/Business: Analytics to advisory—IBM's AI for Finance (2 months); roadmap to "risk oracle" via CFA AI modules, hedging automation with holistic forecasts.

Education/Training: Lecture to lab—FutureLearn's EdTech Design (8 weeks); build "learning architect" blueprints, integrating adaptive platforms for 25% curriculum clout.

AI SKILLS

Field forecasts favor the forward: Scan your sector, select a roadmap—strategic steps to surf the swells.

Proactive Pivots

Pivots demand precision—certs as your cartography, charting from current to cresting. Google's AI Essentials, a 10-hour 2025 staple, kicks it off: Free, foundational, it demystifies prompts and ethics, badging you for resumes that resonate. Follow with Coursera's AI for Everyone (Andrew Ng's gem, 6 hours)—strategic scans of societal stakes, priming for hybrid hires. For depth, IBM's AI Engineering Professional Cert (3 months, $49/month) wires you for workflow weaves, landing "AI integrator" interviews at 30% higher callbacks.

Mid-career? Stack sector-specs: Finance pros grab Wharton's AI Strategy (4 weeks, $79); creatives claim Adobe's Generative AI Cert (2 weeks, free trial). The tactical? Time-box: Week 1 audit (skills gap via LinkedIn's AI matcher), Week 2 enroll, Month 2 project (build a portfolio bot). Platforms like Udacity nano-degrees (3-6 months) bundle mentorship, turning theory to tangible—grads report 40% faster transitions.

Case etched in effort: Marcus, 45, a logistics manager in Chicago, 2024's his crossroads—warehouse bots nipping at his notes. No panic; proactive plot: Starts with Google's Essentials (badged in a weekend), layers IBM's supply-chain AI track (8 weeks, virtual labs simulating drone fleets). Pivot point? Capstone: An AI-optimized route optimizer, slashing mock delays 35%—portfolio gold. By summer 2025, he pitches "Logistics AI Lead" to a green logistics firm; lands at $140K, 25% bump, remote from his lake house. "Wasn't a leap," he reflected over LinkedIn coffee, "a ladder—certs as rungs, case as climb." His secret? Peer pods via Reddit's r/AIReskill—accountability amps completion 50%. Pivots like **Marcus's prove:** Not age-locked, but action-led—strategic certs as your slingshot to sectors surging.

AI SKILLS
Proactive isn't prophetic; it's prepared—enroll in one this quarter, watch the wavefronts welcome you.

Opportunity Lens

Change isn't chaos—it's choice, the lens that reframes automation as your authoring arc. Displacements? Doorways to domains undreamt. Creations? Canvases for your craft. WEF's net 78 million? Your invitation to author among them—reskill not from scarcity, but sovereignty. Lens it thus: Every forecast a fork, every pivot your pen.

Future mapped? Now, in Chapter 15, build bold confidence: Real-world wins from 2025's frontlines.

Chapter 15:

BUILDING CONFIDENCE WITH AI

Doubt's the thief that picks your creative pockets, but in the AI age, confidence is currency you mint yourself—one messy experiment at a time. This chapter's your hands-on forge: Personal play, no pitches or profit chases, just the raw thrill of creation to build that inner "I got this." We'll embrace the experiment ethos that turns tinkering into trust, unpack a playbook of beginner builds like chatty sidekicks, reframe failure as your sharpest teacher with iteration tales, and lock in momentum with simple logs that stack wins. For the weekend warrior prototyping poems or the curious coder cloning clones, this is unscripted alchemy: AI as your sketchpad, not scriptwriter. By the end, confidence won't whisper—it'll wing it, ready for whatever wild idea strikes next.

Confidence Through Creation

Confidence isn't a crown you claim—it's calluses from creation, the quiet grit that grows when you hit "generate" without a guarantee. In 2025, with tools as accessible as your browser, the ethos is simple: Experiment freely, fail forward, own the output. It's not about perfection; it's permission to probe—treating AI as a jam session, not a judge. Why? Because hands-on hacks rewire your brain: Each prompt you tweak, each glitch you grin through, chips away at "what if I'm wrong?" and carves "watch what happens."

Think of it as creative cardio: Low-stakes reps that ramp resilience. Start with whimsy—a Grok riff on "my coffee as a superhero"—and watch doubt dissolve into delight when it spins a latte-lifting origin story. Studies from Adobe's 2025 Creator Pulse echo this: Folks logging weekly AI experiments report 45% higher self-efficacy, that "I can shape this" surge. It's personal, not performative—no audience, just you and the machine mirroring your moves back, bolder.

My own ethos evolved here: Early experiments felt like flailing—garbled images, off-key tunes—but each "try again" tallied trust. Now, it's ritual: Sunday sketches with Midjourney, no endgame, just the flow. The magic? Creation compounds— one doodle sparks a dozen, turning "I'm no artist" into "I'm iterating." Embrace it: Set a "no-delete" rule for outputs, journal the joy (or jank). Confidence blooms not from flawless firsts, but from fearless fiddles—your lab, your rules, your rise.

Project Playbook

Hands-on is where confidence crystallizes, so let's playbook it: Bite-sized builds that scaffold from spark to "see, I built that." These are personal playgrounds—custom chatbots for your quirky queries, not client crushers. Start simple: No-code havens like Bubble or Voiceflow let you drag-drop a "Dream Decoder" bot—prompt it your nightmare ("Flying elephants in fog"), get Freudian funbacks laced with your lore (feed it fave books first). Hour one: Sketch intents ("Interpret symbols"); hour two: Test loops ("What if I add mood sliders?"). Boom—your bedside oracle, confidence cashed in clicks.

Level up to code-lite: Replit's AI pair-programmer co-pilots a "Mood Mixer" app—input "rainy day blues," output playlist + poem, powered by Spotify API stubs. Tutorials? Grok's got 'em: "Walk me through a beginner JS mood bot." The ethos: Prototype in a pomodoro, polish in play—failure's just flavor.

For structured spark, dive this 30-Day Challenges table—daily doses, escalating ease to epic, all solo-sourced:

Day Range	Challenge Theme	Build Brief & Tools	Confidence Boost
1-7: Sparks	Daily doodles—AI image evolutions.	Midjourney prompts: "My pet as pirate, v1-3 iterations." Free tier.	"I shaped the surreal"—visual vocab expands.
8-14: Chat Chums	Personal bots for banter.	Voiceflow: "Recipe roulette from fridge pics." Upload snaps, train responses.	"It gets me"—relational rapport with code.
15-21: Tune Twists	Music mashups from moods.	Suno: "Bluesy ballad from 'lost keys' prompt," remix thrice.	"Harmony from hunch"—sonic self-expression unlocked.

AI SKILLS

Day Range	Challenge Theme	Build Brief & Tools	Confidence Boost
22-28: Story Spins	Narrative nests—branching tales.	Sudowrite: "Choose-your-adventure from coffee spill mishap." 500 words/day.	"Plot power"—narrative nerve, no notes needed.
29-30: Fusion Fest	Hybrid haven—art + audio + app.	Grok + Teachable Machine: "Gesture to generate poem-to-tune." Gesture-train, export.	"My mashup magic"—multimodal mastery, full-circle flair.

These aren't assignments; they're adventures—tweak for your tempo (e.g., swap bots for beats if you're aural). In trials, participants clock 60% more "flow states," that immersive "time flew" where confidence coalesces. Pick Day 1 today; by 30, you'll have a gallery of "mine"—tangible proof you're the maker.

Failure as Feedback

Creation's curveball? The crash that catapults—failure not as full stop, but feedback loop, the gritty grind that gilds your game. Iteration's the incantation: Botch it, break it down, build back bolder. Stories abound: That first chatbot spitting sarcasm at sympathy prompts? Not flop—fodder for finer tuning ("Add empathy anchors: 'That sounds tough—tell me more'"). Each error's an echo, etching expertise: Midjourney's muddy merges teach "layer light first," Suno's sour notes nudge "specify scale before style."

The ethos: Normalize the nope. 2025's creator commons, from DeviantArt forums to Grok guilds, buzz with "fail tales"—posts like "My AI novella bombed on plot holes; pivoted to poetry prompts, now viral verses." It's communal catharsis: Share the shank, spark the shine. Psych backs it—Harvard's

2025 grit study links "failure forensics" (post-mortems with "What worked? What wobbled? Wild tweak?") to 50% faster skill spikes, turning trepidation to tenacity.

Anecdote from the ashes: My 2024 side quest—a "Zen Journal" app, AI-fueled mood tracker promising daily wisdom. Debut? Disaster: Prompts pulled platitudes ("Breathe deep"—duh), UI a usability nightmare (buttons buried in bot blurbs). Beta buddies bailed: "Feels fake." Feedback flood: Friends flagged "too generic—infuse your voice," tech pal poked "Simplify: One-tap zen." Iteration immersion: Week 1, scrap scripts for story seeds ("Today's snag? Spin as fable"); Week 2, no-code revamp via Adalo, ditching dross for doodle inputs. Third try? "Zen Zinger"—user sketches a squiggle, AI alchemizes into personalized parables ("Your loop? A river's reminder: Meanders make the music"). Launched on itch.io: 500 downloads, rave reviews—"Feels like a friend who gets my mess." From botched beta to bestseller stub (self-pub e-book tie-in netted $2K), it wasn't magic; it was method—fail as forge, each flop fueling the final form. Yours? Next glitch, grid it: "Glitch log: What? Why? Wild fix?" Failure's not foe—it's the feedback that frees your fire.

Momentum Makers

Momentum's the multiplier—small wins stacked like sparks to sustain the blaze. Makers? Win logs: A pocket ledger (Notion note or phone jot) for "Today's creation: What clicked? What carried?"—e.g., "Chatbot quip cracked me up; carried to dinner chat." Weekly weigh-in: "Three takes? Two treasures?" It turns ephemera to evidence, that "I'm accumulating awesome" anchor. Habit hack: End-day echo, no judgment—just jot. Over months, it morphs from diary to dynamite, confidence cascading.

Confident creator? Now, in Chapter 16, scale to business: From side sparks to streams that sustain.

Chapter 16:

AI for Small Businesses

Running a small business in 2025 feels like captaining a dinghy in a sea of supertankers—agile, but outgunned on scale. Enter AI: Your secret ballast, leveling the waves so you don't just survive, you surge. This chapter's operational playbook: Growth tactics tuned for SMBs, no fluffy branding fluff—just the nuts-and-bolts boosts that turn tight margins into tidal lifts. We'll unpack AI's undeniable advantage for the little guys, core apps like CRM that crank efficiency, a phased roadmap to rollout without revolt, and checks to sustain the steam. For the café owner crunching comps or the boutique boss battling backlogs, this is your edge without the empire. By the end, AI won't be an add-on—it's your operational oxygen, fueling blooms that outpace the behemoths.

SMB AI Advantage

Small businesses aren't just adopting AI—they're owning it, flipping the David-vs.-Goliath script with tools that punch way above their payroll weight. In 2025, the stats scream symmetry: A Thryv survey clocks a 41% surge in AI uptake among SMBs, with 63% deploying it daily and 58% reclaiming over 20 hours weekly for strategic sails. That's not incremental; it's insurgent—Goldman Sachs pegs 81% of owners viewing AI as essential for the next five years, projecting a 35% growth edge over non-adopters through smarter ops and sharper forecasts.

The advantage? Scale without sprawl. Giants like Amazon hoard data moats, but SMBs wield nimble no-code nukes—Zapier zaps that sync inventory across Etsy and Shopify in minutes, sans IT armies. A Salesforce pulse shows 71% planning AI hikes, closing the chasm: Where corporates lag on legacy locks, you pivot prompt-fast, testing trend-spotters that tease tomorrow's hot seller while they debate dashboards. It's operational osmosis: AI absorbs grunt (email triage, lead logs), exhaling insights—demand dips flagged before stock sinks, customer quirks crunched into custom care.

I've consulted corner stores turned contenders: One florist, pre-AI, guessed blooms; post? Predictive petals via Grok, nailing peaks 90%—revenue ripened 28%. The edge evens odds: SBA spotlights small firms "closing in," with AI adopters outpacing peers 25% in agility metrics. No boardroom bloat needed; your advantage is immediacy—deploy today, dominate tomorrow. In a year where 92% of Main Street's on the train, staying sidelined isn't strategy; it's surrender. Lean in: AI's your equalizer, turning underdog into uppercut.

Core Applications

Core AI apps for SMBs aren't sci-fi suites—they're surgical strikes on ops pain points, starting with CRM that reads rooms like a mind reader. HubSpot's AI in 2025? A lead whisperer: Auto-scores inquiries ("Hot handyman hunt? Nurture with DIY tips"), segmenting lists with behavioral breadcrumbs—open rates spike 40%, conversions climb 25% without cold-call chills. It's not lists; it's lifelines—predictive plays like "This churn risk? Ping personalized perks pre-poof."

Inventory's next intel: TradeGecko or Cin7's AI forecasts "Restock widgets Wednesday—holiday hum inbound," slashing stockouts 35% and surpluses that sink shelves. Pair with QuickBooks' AI audits: "Anomaly alert—vendor variance up 12%; renegotiate?"—cash flow fortified, not fumbled.

Email ops? Superhuman's triage turns inboxes to intel hubs: "Prioritize these 5; draft replies laced with last-buy nods." For service SMBs, Calendly's AI slots "No-show Nora? Resuggest with recaps"—utilization up 20%. These cores compound: A McKinsey scan shows AI-CRM hybrids yielding 30% efficiency edges, turning transactional to transformational.

Case brewed in beans: Mia's Corner Café, a 2024 solo spot in Seattle slinging lattes to locals. Ops overload—manual roasts guessed demand, waste wilted 15% of brews, foot traffic flatlined. Core pivot: Demand forecasting via xAI's Grok-integrated app (no-code plug to POS data). Prompt: "Crunch last quarter's footfall + weather + events—project next week's pour-overs." Outputs? "Espresso eclipse Thursday—double dark roast." Phased in: Week 1 trials trimmed toss-outs 40%; Month 2, layered CRM for "VIP Vanilla? Auto-coupon on lull days." Result? From one outpost to three by Q4 2025—chain sans chaos, revenue roasted 55%, staff steady at five. "AI didn't brew the buzz," Mia mused over macchiatos, "it balanced the books so I could." Her hack? Start CRM-simple, scale to supply smarts—cores that core your growth.

These apps aren't overhauls; they're overdrives—pick one pillar (CRM for clients, forecasting for flow), plug in, propel.

Implementation Roadmap

Roadmaps aren't rocket science—they're ramps: Phased rollouts that ease AI into ops without ops revolt.

Phase 1: Audit and align (Week 1-2). Map must-haves—"Where's the bottleneck? (E.g., lead leaks? CRM it.)"—then pilot one app free-tier. Score fit: "Does it shave 10% time? Greenlight."

Phase 2: Integrate incrementally (Month 1). No big bang—stagger stacks: Week 1, CRM sync to email; Week 2, add inventory feeds. Train tribe: 15-minute "prompt parties" ("Ask Grok: Optimize our rush-hour rota"). Monitor mini: "Pre-AI close rate? Post? Pivot if <15% lift."

Phase 3: Optimize and expand (Month 2-3). Layer loops: "Forecast flops? Tweak data inputs." Automate audits—Zapier zings "Weekly win report: Hours saved?" Scale safe: From solo CRM to full-suite, cap at three tools to dodge dashboard drown.

The guardrail? ROI calculators—your north star for "worth it?" Here's a bullet blueprint, plug-and-play in Sheets:

Time Saver Tally: Inputs: Hours/week on task pre-AI (e.g., 5 on leads). Post: 2. Formula: (Pre - Post) x Hourly Wage x 52 = Annual Free-Up ($10K? Green).

Conversion Crunch: Track: Leads in/out. AI boost: +20%? Calc: Extra Sales x Margin = Revenue Ripple ($15K? Scale).

Waste Watcher: Inventory: Spoilage cost pre ($2K/month). Post: 30% drop? Savings: (Pre x Reduction) x 12 = Yearly Yield ($14.4K? Lock in).

Utilization Uplift: Staff hours billable pre (70%). Post: 85%? Gain: (Post - Pre) x Team Size x Rate x 52 = Profit Pulse ($20K? Expand).

Quick-Quip Quotient: Custom, "Prompt ROI—queries/month x Time Saved/Query x Value/Hour." For Mia's café: 50 forecasts x 10 min saved x $50/hr = $4K/month magic.

Roadmap's rhythm: Audit, adopt, assess—quarterly resets keep it rolling. In my SMB steers, phased firms hit 25% ROI in 90 days; rushed ones? Revert roulette. Yours? Phase one today: One app, one calc—watch the wins waterfall.

Sustainability Check

Sustain the surge? Measure monthly: Dash metrics (e.g., "AI-attrib growth: 15%?") via tools like Google Analytics AI hooks, adapt on anomalies ("Churn creep? Re-prompt CRM"). Quarterly quests: "Team tuned? (Survey: 80% ease?)"—tweak training if not. It's adaptive autopilot: Check, course-correct, compound—ensuring AI's your tailwind, not temp fix.

Business blooming? Now, in Chapter 17, brand it: From ops to outreach that owns the orbit.

Chapter 17:

PERSONAL BRANDING WITH AI

In the AI age, personal branding isn't a megaphone—it's a mirror, polished to reflect your truest self while reaching farther than ever. Gone are the days of polished facades; 2025 demands authenticity amplified, where tools tease out your voice without drowning it. This chapter's your craft kit: Positive pathways to online presence, from content sparks to audience alchemy. We'll explore how AI elevates genuine you, aids creation across platforms with smart generators, boosts engagement via timing tweaks, and refines your signature style. For the thought leader threading LinkedIn or the creator curating carousels, this is empowerment, not emulation—AI as your echo chamber, bouncing back bolder. By the end, your brand won't broadcast; it'll beacon, drawing connections that click.

Branding in the AI Age

Personal branding in 2025 thrives on the tension-release of tech and truth: AI amplifies authenticity, turning "me" into a movement without manufacturing it. It's not about faking fluency; it's forging it—tools that sift your stories into shareable gold, ensuring your quirks cut through the noise. Forbes' 2025 trends spotlight this: Hybrid visibility (remote reps via reels) pairs with AI's "authenticity engines," where 88% of marketers lean on gen AI for daily drafts, yet 92% prioritize "human-first" hooks to hook hearts. The payoff? A Human to Brand survey reveals 44% of employers hire based on branded content—your TikTok thread on "pivot pains" could seal the six-figure nod—while 54% nix mismatches, underscoring the stake: Brand bold, or blend in.

AI's amp? It democratizes dazzle. Once, pros polished profiles; now, free tiers like Grok riff "Elevate my bio: Blend 2025 AI skeptic to strategist, witty edge." Output? A 150-char gem that lands laughs and leads. Or video virality: Descript's AI clones your cadence for clip edits, letting introverts intro without impostor itches. The era's ethos, per Chris Ducker's trends? Video-first authenticity—raw riffs over rehearsed reads—fueled by AI's "community curators" that nudge niche nets (e.g., "Micro-influencer pods for edtech dreamers"). I've seen it spark: A client's "quiet quit" confessional, AI-timed for peak scrolls, snowballed to 5K follows, freelance floods. Branding here isn't broadcast—it's becoming, AI as your authenticity accelerator, turning solo signals into symphony.

Content Creation Aids

Content's the currency of connection, and AI aids turn blank slates into branded blueprints—starting with LinkedIn post generators that ghostwrite your genius.

AI SKILLS

Taplio's 2025 suite? A thought-leader's whisper: Feed it "Core value: Curiosity in chaos," and it spins a carousel: Slide 1 hook ("Ever felt AI's a black box? Unlock it."), Slide 3 stat ("92% biz invest per DMI"), Slide 5 CTA ("DM your 'what if'"). Scheduled seamless, voice-vetted—86% users report 3x engagement, per Skrapp.io benchmarks. Or AuthoredUp: Formatting finesse with AI outlines ("Structure as problem-pivot-proof"), auto-emojiing for eye-pop without emoji overload.

Beyond LinkedIn, aids adapt: Jasper for long-form ("Blog on branding booms—infuse my anecdotes"), Claude for concise ("Tweet thread: 5 AI authenticity tips, punchy prose"). These aren't copy-paste; they're co-pilots—prompt "Refine for my wry wit: Add a coffee quip"—yielding yours, amplified. Buffer's AI scheduler suggests "Post at 8 AM Tuesdays—your tribe's tea time," blending creation with cadence.

To strategize per perch, here's a Platform Strategies table—tactics tuned for 2025's turf:

Platform	AI Aid Spotlight	Strategy Spark & Steps	Expected Amp
LinkedIn	Taplio generators (posts/carousels)	1. Prompt core story. 2. AI-outline 5-slides. 3. Voice-tweak. Post weekly—target pros.	2x connections; 44% hire boost per surveys.
X (Twitter)	Copy.ai thread builders	1. Seed hook tweet. 2. AI-chain 4 replies w/ polls. 3. Hashtag harvest.	40% impression jump; viral virality via trends.

AI SKILLS

Platform	AI Aid Spotlight	Strategy Spark & Steps	Expected Amp
		Thread bi-weekly.	
Instagram	Canva Magic for Reels/stories	1. Mood-board input. 2. AI-gen visuals + captions. 3. Music-match. Story daily, Reel thrice weekly.	25% follow surge; micro-niche magic.
TikTok	Descript AI clips (voice/editing)	1. Script snippet. 2. AI-dub +	50% algo favor;

Platform	AI Aid Spotlight	Strategy Spark & Steps	Expected Amp
		effects. 3. Trend-tag. Duet daily for dupe-free dazzle.	authenticity edges out.
YouTube	Jasper script + thumbnail gen	1. Topic tease. 2. AI-full script w/ timestamps. 3. SEO-slug. Upload bi-weekly, shorts daily.	30% sub growth; long-tail loyalty.

These aids aren't automats; they're apprentices—start with one platform, one prompt weekly. Creators clock

35% faster output, per Medium's 2025 roundup, freeing bandwidth for the bold: Your brand's beat, AI-beating the drum.

Audience Engagement

Engagement's the heartbeat of branding—pulse quickens when AI analytics time your touch, turning scrolls to sparks. Tools like Hootsuite's 2025 Insights now predict "Your crowd peaks Wednesdays 7 PM—post pivot prompt then?"—slicing sentiment from comments ("Curiosity cluster: 60% crave case studies"), suggesting replies like "Love that angle—here's my 2024 flop-to-flow thread." Result? Response rates ripple 28%, as per SurveyMonkey's AI marketer pulse, fostering forums not feeds.

Or Sprout Social's AI listener: Maps "Mention momentum: #AIethics up 15%—jump in with your take?" It clusters convos, curating "Engage these 5: Shared skeptic stories," with canned crafts ("Echoing your echo—my ethics oath QR inside"). No spray-and-pray; it's surgical—analytics alchemizing data to dialogues that deepen.

Case crescendo: Zara, a zero-to-hero edtech whisperer in Toronto, 2024's her blank canvas—LinkedIn lurker, 200 follows, whispers lost in wind. Engagement epiphany: Taps Podawaa's AI selector ("Target: Mid-career makers, 10K reach"), timing posts for "teacher Tuesdays" via analytics ("80% active 6-8 AM"). Content? RedactAI gens hooks ("AI: Ally or alibi? My classroom chaos tale"), but Zara's zest seals: Personal polls ("Prompt fail or win? Vote!"). Momentum mounts: Month 1, 1K interactions via threaded teases; Month 3, collabs cascade—guest spots on ed-pods, affiliate arcs. By fall 2025? 10K tribe, TEDx nod, newsletter nestling 2K subs. "AI didn't audience me," Zara shared in a live, "it amplified my asks—now they ask back." Her hack? Weekly "Engage audit": Top three threads, three tailored touches—turning metrics to magnetism, from echo chamber to echo effect.

Engagement evolves empires: Dial one tool this week, decode your data—watch watchers become walkers-with-you.

Signature Style

Style's your sonic signature—AI refines, but you resonate. Aids like Grammarly's 2025 Tone Tuner scan "Wry? Warm it 20%," yielding "Skepticism with sparkle" scripts that sing you. Refine ritual: Monthly "Voice vault"—collect 10 outputs, score "Me-meter: 1-10?" Tweak prompts ("Infuse irony, nix jargon") till it hums harmony. It's not mimicry; it's mastery—your brand's baseline, AI as the bellows.

Branded boldly? Now, in Chapter 18, manage the shadows: From shine to safeguards that sustain.

Chapter 18:

Managing Risks and Limitations

AI's a rocket booster for your ambitions, but like any engine, it has blind spots—hallucinations that hallucinate havoc, dependencies that derail if unchecked. This chapter's your safeguard suite: Practical error-handling protocols to keep risks reined, no hand-holding on how-to-learn basics. We'll dissect inherent limits with 2025's stark stats, radar up detection methods with a mitigation toolkit, navigate crises via backup blueprints, and embed resilient routines for the long haul. For the operator optimizing ops or the innovator iterating ideas, this is your firewall: Spot the snag, staunch the slip, steer steady. By the end, limitations won't loom—they'll be lines you lead, turning potential pitfalls into plotted paths.

AI's Inherent Limits

AI's prowess packs punch, but its limits lurk like unpatched code—hallucinations and dependencies that demand your diligence. Hallucinations top the glitch list: Those confident confabs where models mint facts from thin air, persisting as a core conundrum in 2025. Benchmarks clock general models at 5-10% error rates for routine queries, spiking to 15% or more in benchmarks testing analytical depth—think a sales forecast fabricating figures that flop your quarter. Newer frontiers fare worse: Specialized tests hit 79% in edge cases like legal lingo or niche narratives, per mid-year probes, where context crumbles under complexity. It's not malice; it's the math—training on terabytes tempts overgeneralization, yielding "plausible" but phony outputs that erode trust if unchallenged.

Dependencies deepen the ditch: AI leans on lifelines like clean data streams and compute clouds, fragile as a single-server setup. In 2025, inference costs have dipped 40% with efficient chips, but outages snag 20% of enterprise runs—think Grok glitches mid-prompt, stalling your strategy session. Data droughts? Models munch on biased bytes, birthing skewed spits; a McKinsey scan flags 30% of deployments derailed by dirty inputs, from outdated datasets to API hiccups. Hardware hurdles hobble too: Edge devices lag on heavy lifts, forcing cloud crawls that compromise speed or security.

These aren't anomalies; they're axioms—limits etched in the architecture. In my consults, a client's chatbot charm offensive charmed zero when hallucinations hawked hoax deals, dipping conversions 25%. Limits linger, but awareness arms: Probe prompts preemptively, diversify dependencies. It's not about ditching the drive; it's driving with dash cams—spotting the skid before the spinout.

Risk Radar

Risks don't roar—they rustle, so your radar's the recon: Detection methods that sniff snags before they snap. Start with sanity sweeps: Cross-check outputs against gold standards—manual mocks for high-stakes (e.g., "AI ad copy? A/B test on a sample squad"). Tools turbocharge: Grok's built-in "fact-check fork" flags 70% of fibs by querying external echoes, while Perplexity's verification layer layers in sources, surfacing "This stat's suspect—source from 2023?" for quick quashes.

Layer in logging legions: Embed audit trails in workflows—Zapier zaps every zap to a Slack channel ("Prompt fired: Output audited?"), catching cascades like chained hallucinations in reports. For dependencies, dashboard divers: UptimeRobot pings APIs hourly, alerting "Grok down? Switch to Claude cache." Bias beacons? Fairlearn's free scanner stress-tests datasets ("Gender skew in hiring sim? 12%—reroll?"), nailing nuances no naked eye nets.

The radar's range? Proactive pings: Set thresholds—"Error rate >5%? Pause pipeline"—via simple scripts in Sheets. In 2025's toolkit, these methods mesh: A Deloitte dive shows early detectors dodging 60% of downstream disasters, from duped decisions to data dumps. Tune it tight: Weekly walkthroughs ("Last week's outputs: Three hallucinations? Hone prompts"), turning radar from reactive to prescient.

To arm your sweeps, here's a Mitigation Toolkit—bullets battle-ready, plug-and-play:

Hallucination Hunter: Prompt wrappers—"Cite sources for every claim; flag uncertainties"—cuts confabs 40%; tool: LangChain's grounding chains.

Dependency Defender: Multi-model multiplex—"Primary Grok flops? Fallback to Gemini"—avoids outages; setup: AWS Lambda toggles, 99% uptime.

Bias Buster: Pre-process probes—"Audit input diversity: Age/gender balance?"—via IBM's AI Fairness 360; remediate with synthetic supplements.

Error Echo: Output oracles—"Rate this response: Accurate 1-10?"—self-score via rubric rubrics; log lows for pattern hunts.

Crisis Cache: Offline oases—"Core calcs cached in Sheets"—bridges blackouts; sync daily for seamless swaps.

Radar raised, risks recede—detection's your dawn patrol, dousing fires before they flare.

Crisis Navigation

When AI's Achilles trips—hallucinated hauls or dependency droughts—crisis navigation's your North Star: Backup protocols that pivot without panic. Core creed: Contingency cascades—layered lifelines from quick quells to full failsafes. First flush: Freeze and forensicate—"Output off? Isolate: Was it prompt poison or data drought?"—then rollback: Revert to last verified version, a Git-like guardrail for workflows (e.g., "Version 4.2 pre-glitch? Deploy now"). Tools temper the tempest: Notion's AI rollback reverts edits in clicks, while Vercel's deploys dodge downtime with blue-green swaps—"Traffic to stable stack, stat."

Deeper dives demand drills: Scenario sims quarterly ("Simulate API apocalypse: Manual mode engaged?"), etching muscle memory. For hallucinations, hybrid hurdles: "AI draft? Human haze-check via peer ping"—a Slack squad vetoes 80% of veers. Dependencies? Diversify decks—"Cloud A down? Local LLM lite"—with Hugging Face hubs hosting offline heavies, bridging 95% of blackouts.

Case clawed from collapse: Late 2025, my client's e-com oracle—a Grok-fueled forecast funnel—flopped spectacularly. Black Friday eve, a data dependency dipped: Outdated supplier feeds fed fibs, hallucinating "Stock surge on socks—order 10K!" Result? Overbuy bust, $50K in surplus sneakers, sales slump as shelves sagged under unsold stacks. Crisis cue: Protocol primed—immediate isolate ("Halt orders: Manual merch match"). Forensicate fast: "Glitch ground zero? Feed fault—hallucination from stale stats." Backup blitz: Roll to cached baseline (last week's vetted viz), cross-crunch with Sheets sims ("Real run-rate: 2K tops"). Recovery rally: Vendor veto loop ("AI alert? Confirm call"), plus prompt purge ("Ground forecasts in fresh feeds only"). Turnaround? Diverted dud to donation drive (PR pop), recalibrated model with debias drills—next quarter? Forecasts nailed 92%, surplus spun to surplus sales via flash sales. "From sock shock to strategy school," the ops lead laughed post-mortem. Navigation nailed it: Protocols as parachutes, turning tumble to touchdown.

Crises crest, but contingencies crest higher—drill your deck, dodge the deep end.

Resilient Routines

Resilience routines are your rhythm—audit habits that harden the hull against hits. Weekly wisdom: "Workflow walk-through: Three outputs spot-checked? Dependencies diversified?"—a 15-minute ritual, logged in a "Risk Recap" doc for trends ("Hallucinations uptick? Prompt polish"). Monthly moats: Mock mishaps ("Sim outage: Backup boot time <5 min?"), plus peer pulses ("Squad scan: Blind spots I missed?"). It's iterative insurance: Tweak thresholds ("Error cap: 3%?"), celebrate clamps ("Nipped 2 near-misses—nail on!"). Over time, routines rout risks, turning vigilance to velocity.

Risks reined? Now, in Chapter 19, assemble your ultimate toolkit: Curated picks to customize your command.

Chapter 19:

LEARNING AI STEP BY STEP

Diving into AI doesn't demand a data science degree—it's a staircase, each step stacking skills without the stumble. This chapter's your core roadmap: A structured progression from zero to zenith, phased for flow, month-by-month with vetted resources, self-assess pivots to keep pace personal, and anchors to sustain the climb. No fluff on why—straight scaffold for the self-starter charting their course. By December 2025, with resources ripened by real-world riffs, this path isn't prescriptive; it's pliable, turning "overwhelm" into "onward." For the bootstrapped builder or the curious coder, it's your sequential spark: Step sure, summit steady.

Phased Learning Model

AI mastery mirrors a three-tier tower—beginner for bedrock, intermediate for builds, expert for breakthroughs—each layer locking in before leaping. Tiers aren't timelines; they're touchstones, ensuring fluency before flair.

Beginner tier (Months 1-3): Foundations first—grasp the glossary (prompts, models, ethics) without equations. Goal: Comfort querying chatbots, spotting strengths (speed) vs. slips (bias). It's unplugged: No code, just concepts via interactive intros, building that "I see it" intuition. By end, you'll craft a simple prompt chain, demystifying the "magic."

Intermediate tier (Months 4-6): Hands-on hybrids—dabble datasets, deploy no-code tools (Zapier zaps, Teachable Machine tweaks). Shift to synthesis: "How does this model mimic memory?" Projects pivot personal—automate a recipe rec, analyze a playlist—fusing theory to tangible.

Milestone: Prototype a mini-app, like a mood-based music mixer, proving patterns over puzzles.

Expert tier (Months 7+): Architect and advance—fine-tune models (Hugging Face hubs), tackle transformers, ethic audits. It's emergent: Lead labs, contribute to repos, consult on cascades ("Chain this LLM for legal lite?"). Goal: Innovate independently, like scripting a custom ethic checker, blending breadth with your bend.

This model ladders logically: Beginner builds buy-in, intermediate ignites iteration, expert empowers invention. Per DataCamp's 2025 guide, phased paths boost completion 65%—no sprint burnout, just steady ascent. Assess at tiers: "Can I explain it to a skeptic?" If yes, climb; if nah, circle back. It's your pyramid—build base broad, peak pointed.

Month-by-Month Guide

Your 12-month map isn't marathon—it's modular, milestones marking momentum with resources road-tested for 2025's tempo. Start slow: Month 1 dives definitions via free feasts like Google's AI Essentials (10 hours, interactive quizzes on basics). Month 2: Prompt prowess with DeepLearning.AI's "AI for Everyone" (Coursera, 6 hours)—non-tech entry, ending with a "prompt portfolio" of 10 tweaks.

Months 3-4: Data dance—fast.ai's 2025 Practical Deep Learning (free, video-led)—jumps to Jupyter joy, no math moats, building a image classifier from cat pics. Month 5: No-code nest, Codecademy's AI track (hands-on, $20/month)—Zapier your inbox, Teachable Machine for toy ML.

Months 6-7: Model mingle—Google Cloud's ML Crash Course (free labs, 15 hours)—deploy a sentiment scanner, then OpenAI Academy's expert modules (community-led, trends like multimodal). Month 8: Ethics embed, IBM's AI Fairness (edX, 4 weeks)—audit a dataset, flag flaws.

Months 9-10: Advanced arcs—Andrew Ng's "Generative AI with LLMs" (DeepLearning.AI,

$49)—fine-tune a chatbot, fuse with RDKit for chem curios if niche nudges. Month 11: Project polish, Kaggle comps (free datasets)—team a tabular tango, leaderboard leap. Month 12: Capstone crown, contribute to Hugging Face (open repos)—your model merged, mastery marked.

Resources riff real: Zapier's 2025 roundup crowns "AI for Everyone" for beginners (non-tech triumph), DataCamp's scratch guide for intermediates (hands-on hero), Google Cloud for experts (deploy dynamos). Pace it personal—20 hours/month max, blending bites (videos) with builds (labs).

To track traction, here's your Milestone Matrix—check off as conquered:

Month	Milestone Marker	Key Resource & Win	Self-Check Spark
1	Glossary grasp—explain "LLM" sans stutter.	Google AI Essentials (free, quizzes).	Craft 5 prompts; do they deliver?
2	Prompt pro—chain 3 for a story spinner.	AI for Everyone (Coursera, 6 hrs).	Output surprises? Tweak to tame.
3	Data debut—load a CSV, spot silly stats.	fast.ai Practical DL (free videos).	Viz a simple chart; insights ignite?
4	No-code nab—build a bot for book recs.	Codecademy AI (hands-on labs).	Runs solo? Share for feedback fun.

AI SKILLS

Month	Milestone Marker	Key Resource & Win	Self-Check Spark
5	Model magic—train a tiny text classifier.	Google Cloud ML Crash (free labs).	Accuracy >70%? Iterate inputs.
6	Hybrid hack—fuse tools for task triage.	OpenAI Academy (community trends).	Saves 30 min/week? Scale a side quest.
7	Ethics edge—debias a dummy dataset.	IBM AI Fairness (edX, 4 wks).	Flags fair? Role-play a rebuttal.
8	Fine-tune flair—adapt an LLM for lyrics.	Generative AI w/ LLMs (DeepLearning.AI).	Outputs original? Remix for rhythm.

Month	Milestone Marker	Key Resource & Win	Self-Check Spark
9	Compete & code—Kaggle kernel kickoff.	Kaggle datasets (free comps).	Top 50%? Peer post-mortem.
10	Repo rendezvous—fork & fix a feature.	Hugging Face hubs (open contribs).	Merged? Mentor a mini-merge.
11	Capstone craft—end-to-end ethic app.	Synth from prior (your lab log).	Deploys? Demo to a doubter.
12	Mastery mingle—lead a local learn-a-thon.	Community cohorts (Meetup/MLH).	Sparks synergy? Seed your syllabus.

This guide's your GPS—detour on delights (e.g., swap comps for chem if curious), but hit markers to momentum-mount.

Pace and Pivot

Pace isn't plod—it's pulse-check personal, with self-assess tools that spotlight stalls and steer shifts. Core kit: Weekly "Skill Snapshot"—a 10-minute mirror: Rate 1-10 on "Prompt precision? Model mojo?" via a Notion nudge or Google Form ("Stuck on stats? Swap to stories?"). Thresholds trigger: Below 6? Pivot prompt—"What sparked last week? Double down"—rerouting ruts. Tools temper: DataCamp's progress profiler (free dashboard, "Your pace: 80% on track?") flags forks ("Theory lag? Jump to Jupyter jams").

Pivot deeper with peer pulses: Monthly "Assess Ally"—swap audits with a Discord duo ("Your build: Buggy or brilliant?"), unearthing echoes like "Overwhelm on ops? Opt for optional overhauls." Or

Kaggle's kernel kernels—scan community comps ("They nailed NLP novices—nudge there?"). It's adaptive alchemy: Not rigid rails, but responsive rivers—adjust for life lulls (parent pivot: Pomodoro parcels) or leaps (aha? Accelerate arcs).

Anecdote from the asphalt: Enter Raj, a 38-year-old retail rep in Mumbai, 2025's his stall-out—Month 3, fast.ai's feeds fried him: "Data deluge, drowning in deltas." Pace plummeted: Snapshots screamed 3/10 ("Math maze—motivation MIA"). Pivot primed: Tool triage—"Snapshot says syntax snag? Sidestep to stories." Swapped stats for Sudowrite spins ("Prompt a product pitch bot"), blending beginner builds with his sales savvy. Ally amp: Reddit r/learnmachinelearning thread ("Stalled on DL? Start small scripts") sparked a "Retail AI" remix—Month 4, no-code CRM classifier from customer chats. Breakthrough bloom: By Month 6, his "ShopSmart" side project (AI inventory whisperer) won a local hackathon, landing a lateral leap to edtech evang—salary spiked 40%, spark sustained. "Wasn't the wall," Raj reflected in a follow-up forum, "the wrong window—pivots pried it open." His hack? "Assess anchors: One win weekly, one wild why." Pace & pivot aren't punishments; they're permissions—tune your tempo, turn stalls to sails.

Self-assess sharpens the saw: Snapshot this Sunday, pivot on a pulse—your path, perfected.

Sustained Spark

Sustained spark's the secret sauce—habit anchors that tether the tower without topple. Daily dawn: 15-minute "AI Ink"—jot one nugget (Notion nudge: "Today's takeaway?"). Weekly weave: "Project pulse"—tweak a tier tool (e.g., "Prompt playground: 3 variants"). Anchor accountability: Cohort commit (Discord duo: "Milestone mail?") or app alarms ("Assess at 8?"). It's micro-momentum: Miss a day? Mercy restart, no masochism. Over years, anchors alchemize effort to ease—your AI arc, ever-ascending.

Path paved? Now, in Chapter 20, stay ahead: Sustained loops for the long game.

Chapter 20:

STAYING RELEVANT IN A FAST WORLD

The world's whirring faster than a quantum qubit—trends tumbling weekly, tools tumbling out, turning yesterday's edge into tomorrow's echo. Staying relevant isn't a race; it's a rhythm, habits that harmonize with the hum without the hustle. This chapter's your adaptation arsenal: External eyes on velocity, vigilance via vetted veins, cycles that cycle in upgrades, and edges to endure the eddy. No navel-gazing on your niche—just the outward orbit, scanning satellites for signals that sustain. For the forward-fencer fencing flux or the operator orbiting ops, this is your external compass: Tune to the tempo, thrive in the torrent. By December 2025, with updates unspooling like confetti, relevance isn't reactive—it's your reset button, pressed proactively.

Relevance Redefined

Relevance in 2025 isn't static shelf-life; it's a sprint in sneakers—trend velocity clocking weekly whirlwinds that rewrite rules before you refresh. Forget annual audits; it's micro-moves, with AI's pulse pounding at "update o'clock" every seven days: Model refreshes like Grok's multimodal mid-December tweak (fusing voice and viz for 20% sharper sims), regulatory ripples (EU AI Act's enforcement edge fining non-transparent firms $10M+), or investment influxes ($2B poured into edge AI for manufacturing, per Amiko's November-December roundup). Exploding Topics tracks 77K+ AI surges, from "agentic workflows" (autonomous task chains up 4,333% in queries) to "synthetic data" (privacy-preserving training data ballooning 2,500%), demanding dashboards that digest dailies.

Redefined? It's external entropy harnessed—velocity as value, where lagging a week loses 15% leverage (Deloitte's Tech Trends 2026 flags 1% of IT leaders "fully agile," the rest rusting). Weekly waves wash in wonders (ChatGPT's in-chat apps for brand banter, per MarketingProfs' December 12 update) and warnings (SEO's Google Core Update clobbering AI-spun slop, Lumar's December dispatch). The reframe: Relevance as radar lock—tune to the turnover, or tumble in the trough. In my feeds, it's fractal: One week's "AI literacy" push (Artificial Intelligence News' December 16 spotlight) seeds next's "continuous education" surge. Redefined right: Not chasing every comet, but charting constellations—weekly recalibs that keep your orbit outer, not outdated.

Vigilance Strategies

Vigilance isn't vigilance if it's vague—it's veins vetted, from newsletters that net nuggets to networks that nod next-moves. Curate a core quartet: AI Weekly's

Tuesday drops (Issue 194's December 9 digest unpacked transformative tech like innovative LLMs, ethical eddies). Pair with AI 4 Planet's global weekly (December 8's key developments: Billion-dollar bets, regulatory recaps). For manufacturing minds, Amiko's end-month memos (November-December's prospects: AI in assembly lines). These aren't inboxes; they're intel infusions—scan 15 minutes at dawn, distill to "Do this: Deploy agentic agents for ops."

Networks net the nuance: Discord's r/MachineLearning (daily dev debates), LinkedIn's AI Frontiers group (exec echoes on trends like Lev Selector's December 12 YouTube: Exciting news from model merges to market moves). Weekly weaves: "Watercooler Wednesdays"—post one nugget ("This week's wild: OpenAI shopping?"), harvest replies for ripples. It's external osmosis: Feeds from forums like MarketingProfs' AI Update (December 12: ChatGPT apps in convos). The strategy sings when siloed: RSS rivulets (Feedly funneling Exploding Topics' 77K trends).—no noise, just nodes.

AI SKILLS

To daily-dose it, here's your Bullet: Daily Scans—rituals that radar the rush:

Dawn Digest (5 min): Newsletter nibble—AI Weekly's top three ("Model launch? Mandate for my stack?").

Midday Mingle (10 min): Network nudge—LinkedIn like/comment on one trend post ("Echo: This ethics edge—how's it hit your hub?").

Dusk Download (10 min): Deep dive one—"YouTube update? (Lev's December 12: Slides on GDrive for seismic shifts)." Jot "Juice: Apply to Q1?".

Evening Echo (5 min): External export—tweet thread or Slack share ("This week's wave: AI in SEO per Lumar—link legs?").

Wildcard Watch (Weekend 20 min): Wildcard web—Exploding Topics' ai-topics (77K surges: Spot "synthetic data" spike, strategize).

Vigilance vaults you vertical: A client's ops orbit, pre-newsletters, lagged 20% on latency; post? Proactive plugs, 35% velocity. Strategies aren't scans; they're sails—catch the current, course-correct constantly.

Improvement Cycles

Improvement's not impulse—it's cycles quartered, reviews that recalibrate against the roar. Quarterly quests: Q1 scan ("Velocity verdict: Weekly waves washed in what?"), audit actions ("Adopted three? Axed two?"). It's external echo: Benchmark against beacons—Deloitte's Tech Trends (December 10: AI leaner orgs, 1% agile IT).—gap your grind ("My stack static? Shift to strategic?"). Cycle core: Collect cues (newsletter nuggets, network nods), cull cruft ("Outdated oracle? Offload"), craft counters ("New norm: Agentic? Agent-ify my alerts").

Reviews ritualize: 90-minute huddles—"Harvest: Highs from last quarter (e.g., AI Weekly's model merge mastery)? Hurdles (Lumar's SEO slop-slayers?)"—then horizon ("Q2 horizon: Exploding Topics' surges?"). It's iterative intake: Not navel, but nodal—external inputs fueling outbound orbits.

Case contrast: Adaptor Alex vs. Lagger Liam, both logistics leads in London's lean lanes, 2025's their split-screen saga. Alex, vigilance vet: Quarterly cycles cued by AI 4 Planet (December 8: Investments in edge AI)—Q1 review: "Manufacturing prospects per Amiko? (November-December: Assembly AI)." Adopted agentic agents for route riffs, revenue ripened 28%. Q2: MarketingProfs' ChatGPT convos (December 12)—integrated in-chat intel, customer churn chilled 22%. By Q4? Ops orbit optimized, ops lead leapfrogged to director, 40% firm faster.

Liam? Lagger's lament: No cycles, just complacency—"Weekly? Whatever." Missed AI Weekly's transformative tech (December 9: Innovative models). Q1 lag: Legacy logs, latency lost 15% market. Q3: Lumar's Core Update clobber (December:

AI-spun SEO sink)—search slumps 30%, scramble sans strategy. Year-end? Stagnant squad, sidelined in shuffles. "Waves washed me under," Liam lamented over lagers. Cycles cleaved the chasm: Adaptors advance, laggers linger—quarter your quests, quarter the quitters.

Cycles aren't chores; they're chargers—plug in periodically, power through perpetually.

Endurance Edge

Endurance edges out exhaustion with buffers baked in—weekly wind-downs ("Scan sabbath: No feeds Friday?"), boundary bots ("Grok guard: 'Remind: Research cap at 7 PM'"). It's external exhale: Delegate digests to digests (RSS roundups), nap on networks (auto-alerts for "must-minds"). Buffer burnout: Batch scans (Sunday surge), celebrate cycles ("Q review? Quiet quest—walk the wins"). Edge etched: Not endless endurance, but elastic—stretch to the surge, snap back stronger.

Relevant always? Now, in Chapter 21, claim your human edge: The irreplaceable you in the machine mix.

Chapter 21:

THE HUMAN ROLE IN AN AI WORLD

In an era where algorithms anticipate our next click, the human role isn't diminished—it's distilled, our irreplaceable traits the secret sauce that simmers synergy. This deep dive celebrates those uniques: Empathy's quiet calculus, creativity's chaotic spark, judgment's nuanced north. No victory laps or wrap-ups—just the profound interplay, where we don't just coexist with AI; we elevate it. By late 2025, as hybrid horizons blur human and machine, these traits aren't relics—they're the rocket fuel, propelling progress with purpose. For the collaborator coding alongside copilots or the leader layering intuition over insights, this is your reminder: We're not replaceable; we're the reason the system sings.

Human Uniques Spotlight

What sets us apart isn't speed or storage—it's the soft skills that stitch souls, with empathy leading the ledger as the ultimate ROI engine. In 2025's hybrid teams, where AI crunches code and queries, human empathy yields outsized returns: A CMSWire report highlights human-AI collaborations boosting customer satisfaction by 25% through that irreplaceable relational read, turning transactions into trust. It's not fluff; it's figures—SuperAGI's analysis clocks empathetic integrations delivering 300% ROI in service sectors, as nuanced nods navigate the "why" behind the "what," fostering loyalty AI alone can't lock.

Spotlight the uniques: Intuition's instinct, that gut-glint spotting patterns in the pandemonium—McKinsey's workplace pulse notes hybrid squads with strong human oversight 40% more productive, as empathy edges out errors in edge cases. Adaptability's alchemy follows, morphing mishaps into mastery; BCG's workforce watch flags AI-augmented teams 20% more innovative when human flexibility flexes around fixed functions. And ethics' anchor: The moral compass calibrating code, ensuring equity in every equation—Deloitte's government gig guide underscores human judgment slashing bias risks by 35% in public sector synergies.

These aren't add-ons; they're the essence—2025's hybrid heartbeat, where empathy's ROI ripples from retention (up 25% in tuned teams) to reinvention (20% innovation leap). In boardrooms I've bridged, it's the human hum that harmonizes the hardware: Traits that don't just fill gaps; they forge futures, making AI's orchestra our opus.

Empathy in Action

Empathy's no ethereal echo—it's action incarnate, the human thread weaving warmth where wires weave wide. In customer crucibles, it's the pivot AI prompts but can't palpate: A Forrester flash from mid-2025 shows hybrid service squads—AI triaging tickets, humans tuning tones—lifting resolution rates 30%, as empathetic escalations ("I hear the frustration—let's unpack that") convert complaints to champions. It's relational radar: Spotting the subtext in a sigh-scripted email, steering solutions that soothe souls, not just symptoms.

Deeper in dynamics: Team tempests, where hybrid huddles hum with human hearths. Microsoft's Work Trend Index (April 2025) spotlights empathy's edge in multi-agent mixes—humans mediating AI outputs, fostering "psychological safety" that spikes collaboration 22%, turning terse texts into trusted ties. Picture the pivot: An AI-suggested restructure risks rifts; the empathetic ear ("What's this mean for your workflow?") elicits insights, iterating to inclusive. It's not scripted solace—AI apes accents, but humans hold space, harvesting honesty that hones harmony.

In creative cauldrons too: Hospital handoffs, where AI alerts anomalies but empathy ensures "How's this landing for you?"—CareMedicus' December dispatch details human-AI duos in clinical cascades cutting miscomms 28%, as compassionate clarifications bridge the buzzword gap. Or marketing melds: Sharp Innovations' September blueprint on hybrid crews notes empathetic oversight amplifying AI ad variants, yielding 35% higher click-throughs by infusing "feels right" finesse. Action's arc: Listen latent, layer lived—empathy doesn't delegate; it deepens, turning AI's data deluge into dialogues that delight. In my hybrid huddles, it's the uncodeable: A team's tension thawed by "Tell me more"—unleashing ideas AI ideated but couldn't ignite. Empathy in motion isn't mimicry; it's the motion that moves us, irreplaceably.

Creativity and Judgment

Creativity's the chaos conductor, judgment the judicious jury—human hallmarks that hone AI's hum into harmonious hits. Creativity sparks in the synapses AI simulates but can't surprise: NovelVox's December deep-dive on synergies shows human ideation in hybrid loops birthing 40% more breakthrough briefs, as wild "what-ifs" warp AI's wired worlds into whimsical wins. It's the lateral leap—AI aggregates, we alchemize, fusing fragments into fresh forms that forums flock to.

Judgment's the scalpel: Ethical eddies where data drowns in dilemmas, humans helm the hard calls. MIT Sloan's February frontier flags human oversight in AI alliances slashing ethical slips 45%, as nuanced "not just now, but next?" navigates net-zero nods or privacy pacts. In creative crucibles, it's the curator's cut—AI generates gallons, we glean gems, judging "Does this delight or dilute?" for outputs that resonate, not regurgitate.

The duo dances in domains: Customer conundrums, where AI anticipates asks but humans adjudicate "Is this inclusive?"—Forethought's synergy spotlight clocks 35% loyalty lifts from judged journeys. Or ops orchestras: AI optimizes routes, judgment jets "But community costs?"—Ruh.ai's December dispatch on hybrid workforces notes 28% efficiency edges when creative calls calibrate cold calcs.

To map the magic, here's a Table: AI + Human Synergies—realms where our uniques unlock unparalleled:

Synergy Sphere	AI's Amp	Human's Halo	Combined Crown (2025 Lift)
Customer Care	Ticket triage, pattern predicts.	Empathetic escalates, builds bonds.	30% resolution rise; 25% satisfaction surge.

Synergy Sphere	AI's Amp	Human's Halo	Combined Crown (2025 Lift)
Creative Collabs	Variant volumes, trend traces.	Intuitive infuses, judges jewels.	40% breakthrough briefs; 35% engagement edge.
Ethical Edits	Bias scans, rule runs.	Moral measures, context crowns.	45% slip slash; 35% trust tide.
Ops Optimization	Data dives, forecast floods.	Adaptive assesses, creative calibrates.	28% efficiency; 20% innovation increment.

Synergy Sphere	AI's Amp	Human's Halo	Combined Crown (2025 Lift)
Healthcare Handoffs	Anomaly alerts, vitals viz.	Compassionate clarifies, judges journeys.	28% miscomm mend; 35% outcome oasis.

These spheres spotlight the splendor: Creativity and judgment don't compete—they compose, crowning hybrids that outshine solos. In my melds, it's the "and" that awes: AI's abundance, our artistry—unleashing uniques that redefine the realm.

Integration Imperative

Integration's the imperative: A blueprint for balance where human uniques aren't sidelined but spotlighted, AI the scaffold we shape. Start with symbiosis stacks—design duos where empathy leads (human helm: "Heart-check this output?"), creativity curates (AI generates, we gem-hunt). McKinsey's January mandate for "superagency" in workplaces urges this: Embed "human veto" in every loop, yielding 40% productivity without the pinch, as judgment jets ethical jetsam.

Blueprint basics: Weekly "Uniques Audit"—map tasks ("AI owns aggregate; I own adapt?"), train tandems (role-play "Bot blunder? Human bridge"). Unicorn Labs' September playbook on hybrid leads prescribes "empathy embeds"—AI alerts laced with "Ask: How's this feel?"—boosting engagement 22% in distributed dynamics. Scale to squads: "Synergy sprints"—quarterly quests fusing fronts (creative fronts flag "Fresh fork?"), ensuring uniques underscore, not undercut.

The mandate's math: BCG's September surge on AI outpacing strategies clocks integrated imperatives delivering 20% innovation in flattened teams, where human halo hones the hybrid hum. Imperative in action: Not augmentation alone, but alchemy—balance as the bold where uniques unlock the unbounded. Blueprint it: Uniques up front, integration instinctive—your world, woven whole.

Humanity harnessed? Look forward, in Chapter 22, to the freedom manifesto: Synthesizing it all into your unscripted life.

Chapter 22:

THE FREEDOM MANIFESTO: CLAIM YOUR UNSCRIPTED LIFE

We've walked this path together—from the wake-up call of AI's quiet revolution to the resilient routines that keep you riding its waves. Now, as 2025 draws to a close on this December evening, let's pause at the precipice, not as spectators, but as architects of what's next. This manifesto isn't a map; it's a mirror, reflecting the freedoms you've forged through mindset shifts, ethical guardrails, and hybrid harmonies. You've debunked myths, built bots, balanced biases—each chapter a brick in your unscripted life. The freedom? It's not abstract; it's yours to claim, one bold breath at a time. With tools in hand and traits unchained, 2026 beckons not as a blank slate, but a boundless one. Ready to step into it?

Recap and Reflection

Cast your mind back to Chapter 1's first flicker: That confession of a layoff-laced laugh, the undercurrent of AI reshaping runs and resumes. We started with demystification—pattern-spotting software on steroids, exploding in 2025's data deluge—then dove into fears, flipping apocalypse tales to augmentation anthems. Mindset minted in Chapter 3's pillars—adaptability's branches, curiosity's itch—paved the way for assessments that uncovered your terrain, roles paying premiums, and prompts that whispered AI's tongue.

From no-code nests in Chapter 7 to ethical anchors in 11, we wove workflows that tamed tasks, sparked creativity without stealing souls, and streamlined services into sustainable streams. Earnings unlocked in 10's landscapes, branding boldened in 17's mirrors, risks reined in 18's radars—each a thread in the tapestry of relevance, from education's pivots to healthcare's horizons. You've reflected on failures as feedback, cycled improvements quarterly, and spotlighted uniques like empathy's edge, where hybrids hum 20% more innovative.

This journey? No linear lecture—it's loops of learning, from phased models in 19 to vigilance veins in 20, synthesizing skills into sovereignty. You've audited uniques, audited outputs, audited yourself—emerging not just skilled, but sovereign. Reflection's reward: The freedom formula we teased in the intro—high income, in-demand edge, unscripted autonomy—now etched in your every experiment. You've claimed it, chapter by chapter; now, live it, legacy by legacy.

2026 Vision

Envision 2026: Not a distant dawn, but your daily dawn—freedoms unlocked, where AI's scaffolding lets you soar unscripted. Picture mornings untethered: No commute's crush, just coffee and code from a cliffside café, your no-code nest from Chapter 7 automating admin so you architect dreams. Income streams from Chapter 10's tiers trickle in passively—a $5K retainer for ethical audits, sparked by 11's manifesto—while branding's beacon from 17 draws collaborators who click, not clash.

Freedoms fractal: Location's liberty, as hybrid harmonies from Chapter 21 let you lead from Lisbon or your lakeside lair, empathy's ROI turning remote rifts to resonant rituals. Creativity cascades unbound—Sudowrite spins from Chapter 8 morph into a side-stacked chapbook, sold on Gumroad without the grind, your judgment's jewel curating what captivates. Time's treasure? Reclaimed from risks reined in 18—weekly audits now whimsy walks, relevance rhythms from 20 weaving wonder without the weight.

Anecdotes illuminate: Imagine Elena, the skeptical parent from our dedication—2025's nap-time nudges now 2026's nomadic homeschool, AI tutors from Chapter 12 personalizing paths while she paints with her pint-sized Picassos, freedoms freeing her fire. Or Jamal, mid-career pivot from Chapter 5's horizons: His AI-orchestrated ops from 16 scale a consultancy to solopreneur sovereignty, quarterly cycles from 20 chasing sunsets in Santorini, unscripted as the sea. You? Perhaps the teacher-turned-curator, ethical edges from 11 etching edtech empires that empower, or the marketer's muse, creativity's chaos from 21 conjuring campaigns that connect continents.

This vision's vivid because it's vested: You've vaulted the velocity, from weekly waves to improvement whirls—2026's not prediction; it's your projection, freedoms flowering from the foundations we've framed. Unscripted? Absolutely—your script, your stage, AI the spotlight.

Call to Bold Action

The manifesto mandates motion: Bold action as your legacy's launchpad, prompts that propel you from page to practice. Start with the synthesis sprint—gather your workbook QR wins from chapters past: That prompt portfolio from 6, the ethical oath from 11, the synergy blueprint from 21. Prompt yourself: "What one freedom from 2026's vision vaults me vertical? (E.g., Nomad's notebook? Nurture it now.)" Bold it: Block a "Legacy Lab" hour weekly—prototype the unscripted, like a hybrid hustle fusing your uniques (empathy's ear on AI's alert) into a micro-mentor circle.

Legacy prompts proliferate: "How does my 2025 recap ripple to 2030's realm? (Mindset's muscle from 3, now mentoring masses?)" Act audacious: Audit your arcs quarterly, as in 20's cycles, but infuse with 22's fire—"Not just relevant; revolutionary." Share the spark: From Chapter 13's collective call, seed a "Freedom Forum"—Discord den or LinkedIn loop—where you legacy-lift, swapping stories of societal stitches (healthcare horizons harnessed) and personal pivots (risk radars refined).

Quote to kindle: As PwC's 2025 AI Predictions closed the year with hope—"AI's $15.7 trillion global boost by 2030 won't eclipse us; it'll elevate the empathetic, the ethical, the endlessly evolving"—let it launch you. Bold action's your brushstroke: Paint prompts into pursuits, like "Legacy lens: What world whispers will my work weave? (From education's equity push in 12 to your unscripted opus.)" No half-measures—commit the capstone: By New Year's, craft your "Freedom File"—a Notion nexus of nuggets (milestones from 19's matrix, uniques from 21's table)—and broadcast one bold beat ("My 2026 unscript: AI ally in [your art]. Who's with?").

This call cascades: Action as antidote to inertia, legacy as the light you leave. You've synthesized the skills; now, script the bold—your era, etched eternal.

Grateful Goodbye

Gratitude grounds us: Thank you for this shared sojourn—from front-matter's invitation to freedom's frontier. You've been the quiet revolutionary I dedicated these pages to—the pivot dreamer, the nap-time innovator.

www.ingramcontent.com/pod-product-compliance
Lightning Source LLC
LaVergne TN
LVHW050930210926
848482LV00013B/590